THE LAW AND THE POOR

ORBIS  BOOKS

MARYKNOLL, NEW YORK

The LAW
and the POOR

Frank J. Parker, S.J.

Contents

Foreword

Frank Parker's proposition that Urban Law as he defines it is an identifiable part of what we call law is quite compelling. Clearly there is a large body of law, or lack of it, that particularly affects urban people who are financially poor in their day-to-day life. If one is poor and lives in an urban area, he or she suffers from, for example, inadequate and unequal housing, employment, educational, consumer, and income resources and opportunities, which deprivations arguably differ to a significant degree from those in rural areas. Urban Law, or the lack of it, is, as Frank Parker notes, being used to assert and to vindicate the rights of the urban poor. For example, there has occurred in the last decade what many have described as an explosion of rights benefitting those who receive public assistance. There has been a similar assertion and vindication of rights on behalf of the urban poor as tenants, consumers and defendants in criminal cases. I say "on behalf of" because, while the urban poor themselves have organized and demonstrated to draw attention to and to rectify their deprivations, in the final analysis it has and will require experts to assert to and to vindicate rights before the courts which are the ultimate arbiters of rights.

Frank Parker points out and properly so that the rights of the urban poor have always existed but that it requires experts—attorneys—to assert and to identify these rights. Unfortunately, because many if not most attorneys engaged in pursuing the rights of the urban poor must concentrate their efforts on a few cases benefitting the greatest number of people, there are insufficient numbers of these experts to go around to assist the urban poor in resolving their day-to-day legal problems. Frank Parker's book fills half of this expert gap—it is meant to and does assist the urban poor person to identify much of the law which particularly affects him or her on a day-to-day basis. I suggest that the urban poor themselves can fill the other half of the expert gap by participating before the courts in the legal processes by which their day-to-day rights are adjudicated. This, I propose, can be accomplished by extending the notion of citizen participation in government to that branch of government which has rarely seen such participation—the courts.

I suggest that one mechanism to achieve institutionalization of citizen participation in the courts would be the establishment of what I would call "citizens advisory councils" to courts, in order to make suggestions to the courts governing all aspects of their administration. I use the term "administration" advisedly because the judicial decision-making function of courts, that is, the determination of facts and law in cases before or likely to come before courts, must always remain insulated from any outside influence no matter how beneficial or noble one perceives the outside influence to be. Aside from this caveat, there remains a great deal of potential involvement by enlightened and informed citizenry in the "administration" of courts. This involvement could include review and recommendations concerning personnel and budget, legislative lobbying for additional personnel and budget and also suggestions about location, redesign or perhaps augmentation of facilities. Another fruitful area of citizen involvement might be efforts to simplify court forms and procedures extending the notion of the small claims forum to higher courts. Especially valuable might be assistance in documentation of what a particular court views as desirable and even necessary substantive law reform. There is precedent and authorization for such activity. Informal Opinion Number 1138 published in 1970 by the American Bar Association stated that an advisory council is not only proper but commendable under the canons of ethics.

In my own state of Massachusetts, our Constitution expressly mandates in Article VI that government officials, whether legislative, executive or judicial, are at all times accountable to the people. I have responded to this mandate by establishing a Citizens Advisory Council to the Housing Court of the City of Boston ("CAC"), a high-level court, which independently of the Court meets regularly and concerns itself with the areas referred to above, especially simplification of the Court's legal process and procedures.

The impetus for the CAC come from my own notions about citizen participation in government but the citizens who have participated have taken to it as ducks to water and stay well clear of my judicial decision-making functions. I suggest that with many counts the impetus might well come from citizens themselves. For example, where judges are elected, citizens might query candidates concerning their views as to an advisory committee; where judges are appointed, such queries might be directed to the appointing authority and, as to appointed judges currently serving, it might be helpful to seek their views.

I commend Frank Parker's book to those who desire to be better informed about Urban Law and the poor and I recommend that all citizens participate in the courts as suggested above if only to round out their knowledge of the law so well presented by this book.

Paul G. Garrity
Judge
Housing Court of the
*   City of Boston*

Chapter 1

The Scorecard

Setting the scene

To most people law is a dirty word. When they think of law, they think of going to jail, or paying taxes, or being forced to do something else that they don't want to do. True, there is this side to the law but there is a friendly side too.

The law can help every American to live better. If we use the law properly, it will be a good friend. However, in order to like someone, we must get to know him. The same is true with the law. We can't use it to help us if we don't understand it. Many rich Americans use the law to help them make money and enjoy a comfortable life. Since American laws are made for all people, there is no reason why poor people cannot use them to help themselves as well. This book will try to explain enough about the laws to help the poor to obtain more benefits from the law than they presently do.

We aren't going to promise 100 percent success for this book. It can't solve many of the problems of the poor because they are nonlegal. In fact, there will be many legal problems that are posed in the book that can't be solved today. The today part is important. In addition to talking about the legal problems of the poor that can be solved today, we will talk

1

about those that can't presently be solved and give suggestions as to what the urban poor can do themselves to begin to put together the start of a solution.

Criminal law will be talked about a lot in this book. Maybe too much. The reader may say: "I am not a criminal. The author must think all poor people are criminals." Not in the least! In fact, given the horrid conditions in most cities, it is amazing that there are so many law-abiding citizens. Criminal examples are frequently used in this book because they are more interesting than examples in civil law. Ask yourself which you read about first in the newspaper: a kidnapping or shipping freight by railroad? Most of our examples on the criminal side apply to the civil side as well. When the laws are different, this will be pointed out clearly.

It would not be right to let the reader think that criminal law examples are used simply because they are more interesting. This is not true. Criminal laws are very important. If ignored, the poor person will be in jail and unable to use civil laws to help himself. Especially with youngsters, it is most important to keep them on the right side of the law. We all tend to try to excuse first mistakes of youth. Hopefully this book will help to guard against repetitions that would be punished more seriously.

The subject matter in this book isn't easy. It would be wrong to hint that it was. The law itself isn't easy. Just as a gambler must cover all bets, the law must cover all possible outcomes. For this reason, it is often complicated. To try to oversimplify is very dangerous because it makes one think that something which is difficult, is in fact easy. This leads to the temptation to try to solve legal problems without the help of an expert. That is guaranteed disaster!

Our aim is to explain enough about the law that you will recognize when a legal problem exists. This isn't as easy as it sounds and it will take us many pages to reach that point. Then, and only then, can we give some solutions that an expert can help you attain and only show other areas where you can help the law itself reach the point where experts will be able to apply the new law in the future. Knowing the terrible state of our cities, we have nothing to lose by trying to use Urban Law to solve our problems. The situation can't get much worse; we will try to show how Urban Law can make it better.

In baseball, there is an old saying: "You can't tell the players without a scorecard." This is also true in writing a book. Unless we are clear as to what will be our subject matter, confusion will arise. There is no better place than the very beginning to draw up the requirements for the scorecard.

The audience

Twenty-five hundred years ago, philosophers in Greece thought of a logical method of attack in order to reach the roots of the subject matter in question. This approach is familiar to us as the "who, what, why, when, where, how" approach. Still in use today, this questioning method will serve us well as a starting point for the study of Urban Law.

A fatal mistake would be to say that the "who" is the urban poor who read this book, and then pass on to the other questions. This would be easy and obvious, but wrong. Why? Because the problems that law (in its most general sense) faces in the ghetto are so widespread and so deep that these problems and any possible solutions affect at the very least all ghetto residents. In a similar manner the teacher, business-man, policeman, politician, or anyone else for that matter who comes into close contact with the urban dweller is also clearly affected by Urban Law. True, the people most involved are the readers of this book; but in a larger sense, the "who" contains all those people with whom the readers come in contact during their day-to-day living. For Urban Law to have a favorable impact, it is necessary that all affected parties be introduced to it and understand its demands, rewards, and penalties.

An important achievement of the recent mass effort at fight-ing poverty in the United States has been that for the first time the opinions of the poor are being listened to, and their complaints are being acted on, more than ever before. For too many decades this country forgot that the poor themselves know the most about poverty and that the start of the solution to the disease of poverty lies within their grasp as well.

There are many fertile areas in which the law can be employed to operate for the benefit of the urban poor. This book will seek to show some of these areas. Laws to help the poor exist; we must understand and use them. It is hoped that this book will be of assistance as well to social workers, teachers, and others who deal with the poor in an intimate manner and are genuinely interested in helping them. For this reason, there is no conflict in defining our audience in general terms.

What is Urban Law?

Now it is possible to pass from the question: "Who is the audience?" to the question: "What is Urban Law?" It is necessary to walk a tightrope on this question. As you will recall, the main difficulty that had to be guarded against when asking who is the audience, was to limit the scope too severely. However, when we look at the subject matter of Urban Law, there is the opposite danger of stretching the definition to such a degree that dribs and drabs from every area of legal concentration would have to be covered. This kitchen-sink approach would tend to make the application of Urban Law principles a strictly hit-or-miss proposition. A sense of unity and direction would be lost as would the specific force of Urban Law as a whole. For this reason, the subject matter of Urban Law must be kept under control. A reasonably full but well regulated body of law will, if properly understood and utilized, gather force and have a snowballing effect in the attempt to bring true equality under the law to the urban poor. However, a large unwieldy mass lacking purpose or force will have only limited, short-range success. Although lack of imagination would be just as disastrous, it is well to recognize at the start that the reins must be kept upon the definition of Urban Law if we truly are interested in genuine, lasting success.

Now that we have restricted our field a bit, it is proper to pose the question: "What is Urban Law?" Possibly a better question would be: "Can Urban Law be defined?" The answer is yes, if you are satisfied with a general definition such as: *Urban Law is comprised of the legal statutes and cases that apply particularly to the financially poor urban dweller in his day-to-day life.*

Granted, a truck could be driven through the holes in this definition of Urban Law. However, as explained, a more broad or less broad definition would not serve our purposes. It should be understood that many of the areas we will cover apply to citizens other than the urban poor. In fact, it would be more accurate to say that only a small minority of Urban Law applies to the urban poor alone. The main body of Urban Law consists in using for the benefit of the urban poor, statutes and cases which were not specifically meant for this purpose. In some instances, these statutes and cases were meant to favor the rich. Urban Law will be a real success if it can use all available laws to help the urban poor, no matter what the original intention of the law or decision seems to be. This then is Urban Law in its most fundamental sense.

Most of the general statements in this book apply to the poor living in the country as much as they do to the poor living in the cities. However, the approach taken to solve a specific problem will be different for a number of reasons. Because of the wide distances and fewer people, lawyers, government agencies and corporations, all use different methods to deal with the poor in the country than they do in the city. It would take too much space to discuss these differences in each particular case. So we will deal with the city poor alone and leave the subject of the poor in the countryside to other authors.

This is a good time to repeat that Urban Law is not taken from a special group of laws that apply only to the poor living in the cities, but rather it is drawn mostly from the whole mass of laws applying to all Americans, rich or poor; city, suburban, or country dweller. It is not that the laws themselves are written to help especially the poor: but rather some of these laws are applied especially to help the poor. A hundred writers on Urban Law would pick 5,000 different laws as being the most important for helping urban poor. Although their particular choices of the most important laws for the urban poor would differ, all the chosen laws would have in common is that they were almost never written for the poor alone. The trick is to use these general laws to help the poor in a very special way.

We must develop a workable Urban Law in the United States. As a country, we cannot long go down the same path that we have walked in the late 1960s. It is a tribute to the great interior strength which this nation possesses that we have been able to weather the troubles that we have suffered in the last ten years. This situation cannot last indefinitely. A nation formed under law and encouraging the free cannot last forever when force and crime replace it as the way to solve our problems.

This gloomy statement is not meant to discourage the insistence on social reform that has gripped this land. In his 1969 Christmas message, Richard Cardinal Cushing, then Archbishop of Boston, expressed the good points of this movement well when he said:

> Every generation has talked of peace, every generation has hoped for peace, but we are witnessing the rise of a generation who intends to think peace and act peace. Peace is not a distant ideal; it is not a vague wish; it is not a hopeless rhetoric—it is on its way, and the reason is simple: man wants it so.

In this context, peace applies to far more than ending war in Indochina. The desire for peace extends beyond wounds caused by guns to wounds that are caused by hunger, crime, prejudice, and other defects in the human condition. In the minds of the younger generation, peace requires as much an end to poverty as it does an end to shooting. There is nothing contradictory in the pursuit of these separate kinds of peace. If an end to shooting wars can be achieved, all the efforts of those seeking peace can be turned toward ending the war in a man's heart caused by poverty. However, as in all laudable causes, there are those who use the wrong means to achieve their goals and those who are more interested in themselves than what they claim are their goals. Great harm of a lasting variety can be done under what seems to be good. Purity of intention is not enough. A man who tries to bail a sinking rowboat with a leaky sieve is good-intentioned; but he is misguided and will surely sink, in spite of his good intentions. This same type of miscalculation of methods is an ever present danger in the search for peace through attempts to eliminate poverty.

The importance of law

It will be a much repeated saying in this book that only through law can America rid itself of poverty. Unless the law is observed, the United States will descend swiftly into a police state. No one can claim that our laws have not been very unfair to some people; however, as this book will show, things are getting better. Without law, this geographical entity will cease to be America. Oh, it may be America in name and location, but not in fact. Look at the laws of any other nation and ask yourself if, with all our faults, our law isn't the best by far. This book will attempt to show that American law, given half a chance, is the only way to achieve peace through the abolition of poverty.

Even more basically, if the law does not help the poor, the solution is to change the law, not change the form of government. The bad experiences of other nations which have changed the form of government rather than the laws are self-evident. It is frightening for us to realize, but America must understand that a very loud minority are really advocating revolution to solve our problems. It is very hard for us to convince ourselves of this fact. However, two minutes of listening to Jerry Rubin or Abbie Hoffman will be proof enough for even the most skeptical. America has revolutionaries who are fully willing to govern by force. We who oppose this must see that the other possibility, use of all our laws, is made as fair and perfect as possible. Urban Law is a vitally important area in this regard. All revolutions feed on the poor to light the flame. Unless a real alternative to revolution is given to the poor, America will follow large nations such as the Roman Empire and nineteenth-century Russia down the path of revolution and destruction. Urban Law is a real alternative to revolution. If it is not, the poor will inevitably be the starting ground for revolution and it will be our government's fault. America possesses the legal structure to guarantee true equality to all. It is necessary that this legal structure be used by the government and all citizens to see that it is done. This is the role of Urban Law. If successful, there will be no revolution. Energy and ability will be all that separate the rich from the poor. Hopefully, Urban Law will put us on the road to this Big Rock Candy Mountain.

Unlike the "who," "what," and "why" categories, the "when" category truly is clear. Urban Law must take effect now. This is not to say that we have not made progress in the past few years. In many areas we have. Wide use of free legal counsel for the poor is a good example. However, on the whole Urban Law successes have been for the most part occasional, not a day-to-day success. There can be no delay. Urban Law must move into action now. There already have been too many riots, too many cases of racial discrimination in all walks of life, too many cases of victimization of the poor, and too many cases of deprivation suffered by American citizens when the Constitution of the United States says it cannot be so. However, it is so. Urban Law must put a stop to this while a structure of law still exists in which it can do so.

Passing on to the "where" category, Urban Law must take effect in both the minds and the hearts of each and every American citizen. Why? Because urban problems affect us all. This is true precisely because the United States is a nation under law. In its fullest sense, this means that every American citizen has the right to receive all the protection guaranteed by our laws. Since this is so, each citizen has the duty to see that every other citizen receives all his rights as well. American democracy is a fraud to the extent that the poor are deprived of their legal rights because of their poverty status. We all must see that law is fairly applied to the urban poor. We are not a democracy if we do not. Each citizen is at fault if he votes for legislators and administrators who permit and even encourage discrimination against the poor. The "where" category is very broad and encompasses the government, corporations, merchants, and organizers be they labor or student in origin, and even extends to the actions of other urban poor. In short, the legal protection for the poor must be as wide and thorough as possible.

Finally, the method to be used in studying Urban Law should be discussed. This seems as good a place as any to assure the readers that there is not the least intention in this book to look down on the poor or their problems. Poverty will be treated as an objective fact. There will be no attempt to assign reasons, blame, or fault. This is not a book in political science, or economics, or social work policy, but only in law. Since a legal approach will be employed, the facts themselves, apart from the factors causing their presence, will be examined and proper legal theories of aid to the urban poor will be explained.

As has been stated previously, Urban Law is mostly drawn from other branches of law. We have always had urban poor, but the reasons and possible solutions keep changing. The man who is poor in the 1970s is poor in a different way than the man who was poor in 1950. A television, for example, would have been a luxury in 1950, but it is a necessity in the 1970s. Examples of what is essential for normal life change from decade to decade. Therefore, the laws that will aid a man in rising above poverty change as well. We must bring the law into the 1970s. The laws of 1950 are not the way to protect the poor in the 1970s. We must streamline the laws.

The next decade contains exciting promise for striking the first telling blow against poverty. If, without bankrupting itself totally, the United States is successful in really aiding the poor, this feat will be in many ways the equal of the first landing on the moon. In both cases, what was done had never been done before. The potential of help to the poor from Urban Law is virtually limitless. This book will try to outline some of these areas.

It would be silly to suggest that Urban Law will solve all of our poverty problems. They are economic and social as much as legal. However, a failure to observe law will take this country down with it. This will end even the possibility of helping the poor. This book has no magic answers. It does not claim to be encyclopedic on the subject. As in any book, the author's stresses, inclusions, and omissions are open to challenge. The purpose is to demonstrate the direction in which law must head in order to solve the problems of the poor.

In the 1920s, a young genius named Watson wrote a book on how to play cards properly in a bridge game. He almost completely covered the field. All books on the same subject for the past forty-five years have done little more than repeat what Watson wrote. There are no Watson's in Urban Law. No one has even 1 percent of the answers. Laws are different in each state. The reasons for poverty are different in each state. The background and living conditions of the poor are different in each state. The attitude of politicians and public servants toward the poor is different in each state. Therefore, no one correct way exists to end urban poverty. It is far more difficult a problem than how to play cards in a bridge game. It would be nice if a book on Urban Law could contain all the answers. It can't because each state, each situation, and each problem is different. The best that can be done is to suggest general problem-solving approaches. More and more, experts are becoming available to work with the poor to solve their legal problems. However, they are too busy to go looking for business The urban poor must recognize, first of all, that a legal problem exists for which they can be helped by an expert. This book will try to discuss many truly legal-problem areas. Then, it is up to the poor, both as individuals and as neighborhood groups, to take the problems to the legal Urban Law experts. This is their field. They dedicate their lives to it. Their chances of obtaining a successful result are better than the layman's. You wouldn't try to repair a broken furnace yourself because you don't know how it operates. So why try to solve urban legal problems yourself when you don't know how they should be attacked? Experts are available (often for free); it does not make sense to ignore them and try to help yourself in a field in which you are not an expert.

This book is not written for lawyers, but for the average city person trying to make enough money to survive. This book will not seek to make lawyers out of nonlawyers; nor will it treat the reader as if he were a lawyer. Clearly he is not and this fact will be emphasized. However, when the poor man on the city street gets to the stage where he knows what the law is, what it demands of him, and what it can do to help him to escape poverty, Urban Law will be on the road to success. Once the urban poor know how Urban Law can help them, they will be able to use it themselves and also demand the government use it to fight poverty.

The goal of this book

The aim of this book is to bring those who read this book to a state of legal knowledge at which warning signals will ring in their head each time a situation occurs that has legal implications. This does not mean that the reader will know the full scope of the legal problem. Even more, this does not mean that as a result of this book the reader will be able to solve the legal problem in question. Just the opposite. The reader would be a fool to try. Nowhere than here is it more true that "a little knowledge is a dangerous thing." There is almost no way that the reader could be right. Law is too complicated. We all fall into the trap of overestimating our own ability in any area in which we can understand the terms used. Think for a minute. What a waste of time and money law school would be if legal problems could be solved without it. The bankruptcy courts and the state prisons are littered with examples of those who found out the truth of this statement the hard way. Lawyers are available. They should be used. There are many urban poor who could be helped by a lawyer and do not know it. It is precisely for this reason that we are seeking to build in an alarm system. Many times people have no idea how the law can be of assistance. It is the purpose of this book to outline some of these situations. Hopefully, those interested will take it from there and obtain legal advice to obtain all benefits of the law to which they are entitled.

Under the laws of this country, the poor man has the same God-given right as anyone else to have the law work for his advantage. Urban Law will give the poor urban dweller this opportunity After nearly two centuries, a new era is beginning for the American poor. The famous line of Captain America in *Easy Rider,* ``we blew it,'' will apply to this country America as well, if we do not help the poor, now.

Summing up

Chapter 1 has been strictly an introduction, so that you won't walk into the subject cold and expect to find ninety-five handy little rules to help you escape ghetto poverty. Books that do this exist. We wouldn't touch one with a ten-foot pole. There are no easy answers. Disbelieve anyone who tells you that there are.

This book will play a role similar to a treasure hunter in the middle of a shipwrecked boat. We are looking for hidden gold; that is, laws that will be of use to the poor in the midst of the shipwreck which is our large cities today. Fortune hunting is hard work; so is Urban Law. However, success awaits the urban poor who use the law intelligently; just as success awaits the fortune hunter who finds gold. It is time to start the treasure hunt.

Chapter 2

Law and the Legal System

Setting the scene

If someone says chocolate cake, everyone knows what he means. Yet the same is not true for the term *law*. It would be disastrous to attempt to talk about law that will help the poor in the city, before we are very clear what we mean by the term law. As we will soon see, there are at least three different, commonly used descriptions for the term. We must clearly label and separate these three different types and make sure we understand exactly what we mean by law for the purposes of this book.

Law in its most general sense

For as long as there has been life existing on this earth, there have been laws. Once two people live in the same area, they must establish ground rules in order to live together without bloodshed. In caveman days, a law might have been no more elaborate than an unspoken agreement that each person will eat the food on his own plate. If either of our cave dwellers in this example began to help himself to the food on the plate of the other, a swift blow with a handy rock would most probably be the response of the offended party to punish this violation of the law.

This is the broadest possible interpretation of the word *law*. Law here means any regulation carrying with it close to absolute certainty that it will be followed. In this sense, *law* applies to virtually every area of life. It is a law of nature that plants will die if not watered. It is a law of rational psychology that when faced with two choices, man will choose the one he thinks is best for him. It is a law of the household that the children put away their toys. It is a law of baseball that there will be nine men on the team.

The examples of law in its most general form are neverending. These kinds of laws are nothing more than *ground rules*. The penalties for breaking these laws are closely connected with these laws. A plant that is not watered will die. Man would become insane if he selected that which seemed less good to him. A child who fails to put away the toys will be spanked. A ball team without nine players must forfeit. In all the examples of law that we have discussed so far, we are talking about nongovernmental regulations with nongovernmental penalties for those who break these laws or *ground rules*. This is not to deny these categories the dignity of classification as laws. This use of *law* in a loose sense does not demand 100 percent accuracy. On the other hand, the probability of success must be high enough that we are talking about more than just high probability. The less formal and less demanding designation as a *rule* is not enough. It is necessary to be selective with the designation of *law*. For example, it is a law that the team who scores the most points wins a basketball game; but it is only a rule that the team with the tallest players wins a game. It is even necessary to be selective with the less exact designation of a *rule* as the following quote from the nineteenth-century English author William M. Thackeray will illustrate: "So many handsome girls are unmarried, and so many of the other sort wedded, that there is no possibility of establishing a rule."

Law as a set of regulations

Law as standing for any sort of usually true set of regulations is much too broad a category for our purposes. We will not use again the first type of law that we just talked about when we refer to *law*. For our purposes, as will be demonstrated, *law* will be used in a governmental framework. The second context in which law is used is the most familiar. It is law as statutes. Each governmental unit has a series of regulations by which it functions and regulates the conduct of those with whom it deals. But who is government? In America, no matter whether we are talking about the city, state, or national government, it is nothing more than a total of all those citizens living in the area covered. A government both protects its citizens from each other and assists them by providing group services that they would not be able to afford as individuals. Therefore, in its most primary form, a government is the people.

In a democracy, the men who work for the government are the representatives of all the citizens. These representatives are elected by all the citizens, or appointed in the name of all the citizens, and are responsible to all the citizens. As part of their representative capacity, some of those who govern have the authority to pass laws in the name of all the people for the purpose of binding all the people. It is within this framework that we traditionally think of the word *law*. To be more specific, but still fatally broad, *law* for Americans is thought of in the federal structure in which Congress makes the law, the Judiciary interprets the law, and the Executive carries out the law. To a large extent, the various state and local forms of government have been set up along lines that are similar to the federal system.

It is within the structure of laws, their institution, interpretation, and implementation, that society must function. It is not necessary to discourse at length about the impossibility of human life in a society without laws. If we need any further reminder of this fact, our memory has to return some twenty-five years into the past to the horrors of concentration camps at Auschwitz and Dachau. Closer to the present, Vietnam, Northern Ireland, and Biafra are all terrible examples of death and suffering. In each case, law broke down. Violence soon followed.

Since the American form of government places such stress on law, it is well for us to consider at this early point the time factor of law. Its importance in this area cannot be over-emphasized. Each and every law in our system comes into effect; or if you wish, is born at a certain moment in the history of our country. To use the federal side as an example, this occurs either when the President signs a bill that has been passed by the Senate and House of Representatives and sent to him for his consideration and hopefully his signature; or when the President takes no action upon the bill in such circumstances as to constitute a signature and not a pocket veto.

There are four ways in which a law presently in effect can lose its force. It can be repealed, or its place taken by a new law, or if when passed it was given a date when it would cease to exist, or if the Judiciary declares it to be unconstitutional. Until the law ceases to exist for one of these reasons, we are bound to follow it exactly as written. This means that all drafts of the bill, all the compromise versions and all that went on in the committee hearings, investigations, reports, etc., and everything leading up to the passage of the bill have no binding effect except to give clues as to what was the intention of the Legislative Branch when it drafted the bill that eventually became the law. We must observe only the words written in the law.

Similarly, for as long as the law is in effect, those who deal with the law—mainly the courts—cannot be interested primarily in the day-to-day change in the nature of the problem. This is true even though the passage of time could tend to make the law less desirable than when it was enacted. This is an important concept that must be grasped. If it is not grasped, most of what follows will not be understood properly. United States Supreme Court Justice Cardoza explained this maxim in a clear fashion in the 1933 case, *Anderson v. Wilson:* "We do not pause to consider whether a statute differently conceived and framed would yield results more consonant with fairness and reason. We take this statute as we find it." In other words, just as Sergeant Friday used to say in the show *Dragnet,* "just the facts, ma'm," here the courts are interested just in the words as written.

It is the Legislative Branch that is charged with the responsibility of keeping our laws in tune with today's world. Of course, both the Executive Branch, which carries out laws, and the Judicial Branch, which interprets laws, also do have an interest in seeing that the laws are up to date. However, the primary responsibility of the Executive and Judicial is to work with the law as it presently is written on the books. Why is this so? If we pause for a moment, the answer should be clear. There would not be a dependable base on which everyone could rely.

Imagine the anarchy that would result if each man charged with first degree murder were charged under a law that kept changing. Suppose Denver had five deaths attributable to drunken drivers running over pedestrians during the month of January. All five were found guilty of manslaughter since the intent to kill that is necessary for first degree murder was missing. If the judge in the case had the authority to say to the sixth drunken driver in January who killed a pedestrian: "You have had it—six deaths by you no-good drunks is too much. The heck with intent. For Denver, this sixth death caused by a drunken driver will be first degree murder and you will get the chair." Naturally, this is an extreme example. Still the idea behind it is valid. It must be recognized that if the passions of the moment can push the law from pillar to post, we have little more than a lynch-mob approach. One of the best features of our system is that the formality and detail necessary for enacting laws causes a sufficient amount of time and thought to occur to insure reasoned decisions that are more than mere spur-of-the-moment decisions. It is for this reason that the law as written is observed until a new one takes its place. This is the only way in which a legal system can survive.

Law as a day-to-day proposition

The third legitimate use of the word *law* has been hinted at in the discussion above. This is law in its environmental sense, that is a here-and-now, day-to-day interpretation of the proper penalties that ought to be available for the benefit of those who have been injured. Man, when he places his mind to schemes that put himself ahead of the common good, can skirt any law that exists. It is necessary that new penalties be drawn up to protect the public against new schemes that work against the general good. Actually, the need to keep laws as current as today's newspaper extends far beyond the simple function of using law to right wrongs. In a positive sense, we must have regulations that are current, in order to solve the new problems that our urban society has caused. Not even the laws of twenty or thirty years ago will solve the problems of today. If one doubts this, he has only to look at a 1950 movie on television. It isn't the same world. Sociologists tell us that with better communication and better research the attitudes of people will change more rapidly in the future than ever before. The turmoil of the late 1960s is proof positive of this statement. Therefore, the legal system must adapt to the new world. Once agreement occurs with the fact that the law itself must come into the 1970s, cognizance is being taken of the environmental element of law. Just as we need fresh air, we also need fresh laws.

Any treatise on law that is worth its salt walks a fine line between *statutory law* and *environmental law*; that is, between the law as it is written and the law as it should be; or, if you will, between the second and third types of law we have discussed. Urban Law almost to a unique degree experiences the gap between the law as it is written (if indeed there is any written law dealing with the problem in question) and the law as it must read to cover the environmental structure of the present-day urban neighborhoods. This book will try to touch both sides of the line; both Urban Law as it is or is not contained in the statutes (i.e., our second definition of law), and Urban Law as it should be written in the statutes if it is to respond intelligently to the present-day needs of the dwellers in the city neighborhoods (i.e., our third definition of law). It is necessary to keep in mind at all times that any possible application of law that will be of real help to the urban poor in the future must be looked at with distrust until actually tested in day-to-day application and enforcement.

There are any number of practical examples that could be used to illustrate the difference between statutory law and environmental law. Because they are clear and easy to understand, three examples dealing with kidnapping have been chosen. The first was a 1950 clothing store robbery (at least that's what the two robbers throught they were doing) in which the store clerk was slightly roughed up by the robbers while they held him at gunpoint. David Knowles and Caryl Chessman were the two robbers. Imagine their surprise when they were indicted for kidnapping on the above facts. California has a special type of kidnapping statute. This type of kidnapping found in Section 209 of the California Penal Code could be violated in 1950 in the following ways:

> (e)very person who seizes, confines, inveigles, entices, decoys, abducts, conceals, kidnaps or carries away any individual by any means whatsoever with intent to hold or *detain* or who holds and *detains,* such individual for ransom, reward or to commit extortion or robbery . . . .

The "detention" part of Section 209 got Knowles and Chessman in trouble. The only "detaining" they did was to hold the owner at gunpoint long enough to rob him. They hardly moved him at all. They were playing for big stakes since a 209 violation with bodily harm occurring could carry the death sentence or life in jail without the possibility of parole. Neither alternative was very appealing. Knowles was tried first. He screamed loud and clear that holding a man against his will, without moving him, was a stickup and not kidnapping. This was not what the law meant by "detention." The court seemed to agree, but claimed that its hands were tied. All the court felt it could do was to go to the statute charged and apply it as written. This it did. The court put in all the elements of the crime and matched them up with the requirements of the statute. Everything fit and the machine lit up, bingo!

The conviction of Knowles for Section 209 kidnapping put the California Supreme Court in a very bad spot. The court knew in its collective heart that Knowles had not committed a crime that deserved life in prison without the possibility of parole. Armed robbery? Yes! Assault and battery? Yes! But Section 209 kidnapping in which robbery and bodily harm occurred? No!

When Section 209 was passed originally in 1901, criminal law was not the exact science that it has become in the last few decades. For one thing, even after giving due consideration to the smaller population base, there were far fewer criminals and crimes in the nineteenth century. Present-day lawlessness has given criminal justice a splendid opportunity to work out all the possible kinds and variations of criminal conduct. No matter what type of illegal scheme a potential lawbreaker could think of today, it is a pretty safe bet that some other crook has tried it before. By 1950, California courts had encountered hundreds, possibly even thousands, more kidnappings than they would have by 1901 when Section 209 with its broad definition of kidnapping was originally passed. By 1950, California's grasp of kidnapping and the elements pertaining to it had reached a point of sophistication at which the properly trained legal mind would rebel at the suggestion that forcing someone against his will to remain stationary, in and of itself, would, except under the most serious of circumstances, constitute kidnapping. Clearly in 1950, and even more so today, to constitute kidnapping, it would be necessary not only to *detain* a person against his will, but also to *move* him to another place against his will. (N.B., the only exception would be a bizarre case such as the Mackle kidnapping in which the unfortunate victim was placed in a box in the ground. This sort of case fits the kidnapping definition because there is an intent to kidnap the victim even without movement.) How much movement is necessary to qualify an offense as

Section 209 kidnapping was not the main question here. Everyone agreed in 1950 that some movement must occur for Section 209 kidnapping. If detention alone were enough for Section 209 kidnapping, every California robber who in any way harmed his victim (even if he gave the victim only a light slap) would be in danger of going to the gas chamber should the district attorney choose to seek a Section 209 indictment. Under this type of reasoning, any "kissing bandit" would be in danger of the gas chamber. Clearly in many of these cases, the punishment would not fit the crime. There would be a serious imbalance in the law. Section 209 has a definite purpose and place in California law, but a situation such as the *Knowles* case is not it.

We can all appreciate the awkward position that the California Supreme Court was placed in by Section 209 when it reviewed the *Knowles* case. It is logical to assume that these justices entertained only the blackest of thoughts for the district attorney and grand jury that so abused their discretionary powers as to charge Knowles under a statute that could bring a death sentence, when he did little more than commit a common, garden-variety type robbery. No matter what the justices thought of the common sense and fairness of the district attorney and grand jury, they realized that they were powerless to help Knowles. The hands of the justices were tied. In a nation under laws, judges more than anyone else are bound to apply the law. This obligation is derived from their very function. Judges are created to settle controversies and apply appropriate statutes. When a judge goes beyond his function and makes his own law in order to decide a particular controversy, he is no longer a judge, but a self-appointed legislator. This is a serious offense. We saw this in the Denver drunk-driving example. A judge is not paid to be a legislator. It is not his function in our democracy. It is up the the legislature to change poor laws. In the *Knowles* case, the California Supreme Court acted in a praiseworthy manner. It withstood the temptation to play legislator and left this duty where it rightfully belonged, with the legislators at the state capitol in Sacramento. With a heavy heart, the California Supreme

Court upheld the Section 209 conviction of Knowles, and sentenced him to life without the possibility of parole. In a country operating under laws, this is all that the group with the prime responsibility for operating under these laws could do.

The California Supreme Court did not pack its tent and go home after affirming the Section 209 conviction. Although its hands were tied in a direct fashion, the Court was able to bring about a solution to the problem in an indirect manner. Using the authority of its office, the Court strongly urged that the Legislature amend Section 209, fast.

The Legislature acted upon the suggestion of the California Supreme Court in swift order. Section 209 was amended so as to require that movement must occur along with detention in order to qualify as kidnapping for the purposes of the section. There is no arguing with the fact that Knowles and Chessman never forced the clerk in the clothing store to move more than a few feet. Probably with Knowles in mind, the California Legislature wrote into the new statute a provision that parole was always possible for a Section 209 conviction to which a life sentence had been given. Eleven years after his trial, Knowles walked out of the San Quentin gates, free on parole. Sometimes it takes the law a long time to get going in the right direction, but given time, it usually gets there. The law is not always an ass, as a character in a book by Charles Dickens once said.

Since John Knowles ended up in jail for eleven years, and Caryl Chessman went to the gas chamber anyway for other violations of Section 209 in which he clearly moved his victims, it is necessary to inquire if all the fuss about dropping the wrongly-brought Section 209 charge was worth it. The answer is a strong yes! As explained, the legal environment surrounding Section 209 had become more refined than the detention provision. By 1950 standards, neither Knowles nor Chessman had committed a violation of Section 209 during the clothing store robbery. The United States Constitution guarantees that a man will be punished only for the crimes that he actually does commit. The fact that Knowles and Chessman were bad customers was immaterial. They were United States citizens like everyone else, and they were entitled to the same protections that were enjoyed by everyone else. Once we adopt separate standards for undesirables, it is hard to know where to draw the line on the definition of "undesirable." Soon we will descend into a state described in George Orwell's book, *Animal Farm* (New American Library, New York, 1971). "All animals are equal, but some animals are more equal than others." Neither in *Animal Farm* nor in America would this be a democracy. The criminal acts actually committed by Chessman and Knowles, before they were arrested, were totally sufficient to insure that justice would be served by punishing only these acts. It was not necessary to stretch the legal environment out of shape in order to see that these men were punished adequately for the clothing store robbery. If they did not truly kidnap anyone during this robbery, it is a failure in our system of justice if they are punished as if they had kidnapped someone.

Not all courts have resisted as well as did the *Knowles* court the temptation to play legislator. In the State of Washington in 1939, another kidnapping case occurred that did stretch the legal environment out of shape, causing a serious breakdown in the administration of justice. A physician named Berry became convinced that his wife had been raped while he was absent from a party which they had been attending. There appeared to be no basis in fact for this belief. However, he beat his wife until she named another guest as the one who attacked her. Doctor Berry rounded up two friends and went to the home of the man his wife had named. The three intruders dragged the accused from his home and threw him into a waiting car. The victim's wife and children witnessed this invasion. In a secluded spot, the victim was beaten and mutilated.

The kidnapping statute for the State of Washington was poorly drawn. A fair reading could lead one to read the law as requiring that a ransom or reward be sought by the criminals in order to qualify as kidnapping. In other words, unless the criminals sought to obtain money, there could not be a kidnapping conviction in Washington. The Washington courts recognized the problem, but instead of applying the statute as written, they manufactured a reward out of thin air in order to comply with the statute. Believe it or not, the court said that the spirit of companionship that Doctor Berry and his fellow thugs gained from banding together to torture the victim was the reward necessary to fulfill the statutory requirements.

This excuse used by the Washington Supreme Court in order to uphold a kidnapping conviction against Berry is very thin. In the legal environment of 1939 in Washington, Berry's act was kidnapping. However, the statutory definition of kidnapping did not fit the facts of the crime. Therefore, it would be necessary to change the statute to conform with the legal environment. It is a fundamental guarantee of our legal system that a man must be tried for offenses committed against the criminal statutes, as then written. If the conduct of the accused did not violate a presently existing statute, he cannot be convicted of this offense. In a nation under law, the defendant must be acquitted if the facts do not fit the statute. It seems a shame to do so. However, the very act of so doing is proof of the strength of our legal system. It is far preferable for a system under law to allow a guilty man to go free because of a loophole in the criminal statute than it is to twist the fair application of the law in order to convict one who has not violated an existing statute. Once a pattern of depriving a citizen of his rights is instituted, it picks up steam and is hard to halt. Soon, this would not be a nation under laws. All men would be equal, but some men would be more equal than other men.

The need to keep the legal machinery well oiled is most important. If it is not done, the day-to-day living conditions in America will outstrip the law and make our laws, as a practical matter, useless. In no area more than in the ghetto is it necessary for this country to keep the second and third meanings of the word *law* in touch with each other. Too often in the past, this was not done. What the law said, in theory, would happen in a certain situation did not occur in practice. The cornerstone of our democracy, equal protection under the law for all, crumbles if this situation long exists.

If the cornerstone disintegrates, the rest of the structure will soon follow. True equality for all under the law demands that the legal statutes and the legal environment remain in harmony.

For a recent example of a laudable attempt to keep the legal statutes and the legal environment in harmony, the 1969 California case, *People* v. *Daniels,* is cited with approval. This case could be subtitled *Son of Knowles*. The factual situations are strikingly similar. On four occasions, Daniels and a partner forced their way into the apartments of women. In each case, the women were robbed and dragged to a convenient spot where they were raped in an especially brutal fashion. Among the charges brought against the defendants, as you might expect, was a violation of California Penal Code, Section 209. However, the California Supreme Court refused to allow Section 209 convictions to stand. In a definite attempt to move the statute up to the legal environment, the California Supreme Court said that the movement involved in these rape cases was not enough for a Section 209 kidnapping conviction. The California Supreme Court did not say how much movement was necessary to sustain a kidnapping conviction under the 1951 version of this statute; but clearly, a few feet will not be sufficient any longer.

In an attempt to summarize our discussion of the concepts of the relationship between legal statutes and the legal environment, it will be helpful to draw back a step and review the progress of California Penal Code, Section 209, over the last twenty years. Before the *Knowles* case, it was not necessary to move the victim an inch to qualify as kidnapping. After the *Knowles* case, the California Legislature made some movement a requirement, but it didn't say how much movement was necessary. They left this question up to the courts to decide. For eighteen years, California courts never really answered this question. When it did face the question, the answer was that the amount of movement cannot be "totally incidental." The question that must be squared away in the future is: How many feet is "totally incidental"?

The reader who is staying with this tale, step by step, would be justified in wondering why one change of Section 209 was made by the Legislature (post-*Knowles*), and why the other was accomplished by judicial decision (*Daniels*). The answer is that the *Knowles* case demanded a change in the wording of the statute (need for more than mere "detention") in order to reach a just result that would be in keeping with the then current legal environment. On the other hand, in the *Daniels* case, the word ("movement") was not in conflict with the legal environment, necessarily. All that was demanded was a clarification of the wording of the statute in order to keep the statute in harmony with the legal environment. This interpretive role is a function of the Judiciary. It is up to the courts to decide how much movement is necessary. Granted, the line between courts interpreting statutes which is praiseworthy, and writing new statutes which is not praiseworthy, is a thin one. However, it is submitted that the cases of *Knowles*, *Berry* and *Daniels* illustrate the difference clearly and demonstrate California's wisdom in this matter, and Washington's lack of same.

Summing up

In this chapter we have attempted to draw a balance between statutes and cases, on the one hand, and the legal environment, on the other hand. When these forces compliment each other, a democracy works. When they do not compliment each other, it is necessary to get rid of the imbalance. Unless this is done, our legal system will not prosper, and democracy, in its true sense, will perish. To say the same thing in another way, the law must be kept relevant. If it is not, a new group will take power with their own laws. It is highly unlikely that we would like their laws as much. Their laws might be entirely too relevant for our liking.

Chapter 3

A Mighty Fortress
Is Our Constitution

Setting the scene

By this time, we trust the reader understands why it is absurd to think that law books have all the answers. Because the application of laws keeps changing, it is impossible to say today exactly how the law will be applied tomorrow. All we can do is to lay out the basic principles and apply them as well as possible as new problems occur. Yet below these basic principles we talk about, is our Constitution. Everything else in America depends on it. Without the Constitution, there is no law, and really there would be no country. Since this is so, we must understand the Constitution's purpose before we move our discussion into the cities themselves.

The personal rights that each American citizen has are the bedrock of democracy. Take away these constitutional protections for the individual, the often threatened nightmare of America becoming a police state would become a reality.

The growth of constitutional protection

In theory, all American citizens have always shared the same rights. However, in practice, it is clear that America has been far closer to Napoleon the Pig's rule in *Animal Farm* than it would like to admit. Just as some animals were more equal than other animals, some Americans were more equal than other Americans. This is a historical fact. Though understandable, it is not excusable in a democracy. All our great talk about founding a brand new form of government in the New World notwithstanding, it must be remembered that most of the founders of this country were descended from British, French, Spanish, or Dutch backgrounds. Although the national backgrounds of immigrants from all these countries were quite different, they all had in common the fact that the nation which they were leaving had a king and noble class as a basic governmental structure. In some of these countries the eighteenth-century rulers had more power than in others. However, in all there was a rich group of special families who possessed the largest share of the privileges. As often happens when a group of people break away from an old way of doing things, the new way of doing things which is established in its place possesses a far closer resemblance to the old one which they wished to eliminate than those who have broken away would like to admit. Two reasons readily come to mind for this strange fact. The first is that any structure that has existed for a length of time has solved many problems of necessity. Some of the solutions have more merit than might appear at first glance. People who wish to change a system often find that although it is very easy to criticize a certain procedure, it is often extremely hard to produce a workable substitute. The second reason why the old system unconsciously resembles the new is that the roots of old systems are planted deep in the subconscious of the founders of the new system. Often without realizing it, there is a tendency to slip back into the pattern of the way of life under which the old system operated. It is true that the colonies needed and set up a new system. Nevertheless, we would be making a mistake if, at the same time, we forgot the European influence of the early days of our country.

The fact that our country came from a European culture explains in great part the preference initially given to white, male landowners. This was the closest substitute for the rich European nobles that America possessed. It is easy to understand why this preference failed to appeal to the Revolutionary War soldiers who did not own land. They had risked their lives for freedom as much as and in many cases more than the gentlemen-officers. Unless democracy applied to the non-landowning foot soldiers in a meaningful way, their lives would be little different than they had been under British rule. The democracy which they had worked so hard to erect would not be a real help to them. Naturally, they resisted the plan to deprive them of their right to vote. They placed enough pressure on the landowners to force them to give up their ideas of attaining a superior legal status to that of nonlandowners. As far as the government was concerned, all white men would be equal before the law.

Shortly thereafter, the original privileged class of white, male landowners was expanded for a second time to give meaningful rights to groups of individuals banding together to form an artificial person, called a "corporation." Formal recognition of this concept came with the important 1819 Uited States Supreme Court decision in the *Dartmouth College* case. From that time on, an artificial person (at this time presumably all white) joined the ranks of those fully protected under the American law. We will talk more about corporations later in the book.

In the wreckage of the War between the States, America made another attempt to bring all its citizens into the preferred class of having all their legal rights recognized. The Thirteenth, Fourteenth and Fifteenth Amendments stated publicly the fact that this country had denied to a substantial portion of American residents the privileges of American citizenship solely because of the color of their skin. Over one hundred years later, total racial equality is still more theoretical than actual in this country. The necessity of a book on Urban Law is clear proof of this point. Since to a large extent poverty and black still go hand in hand in this country, it cannot be denied that in those areas in which law is employed to work hardship against the poor, the 105-year-old guarantee of equality without regard to color is not yet a fact. As the Bible says, "How long, how long, Lord, must I wait."

With all the fame that women have achieved in the last fifty years, it seems hard to believe that as short a length of time ago as 1920, even the most fundamental right of voting was denied to them because of their sex. In a slightly more polite manner, their legal status was only relatively better than that of blacks. When we add black and female together, great discrimination still exists today. Although the recent growth of female liberation groups from the freak state into that of a vocal minority indicates that at least some of the female sex do not feel that true equality has been gained, the situation is certainly much better than it was fifty years ago. Actually, the current complaints concerning inequality seem to be more concerning daily life in general than legal in nature. This is especially true in light of the Civil Rights Act of 1972. This federal statute went a long way toward burying any inequalities that still might exist in the legal status of women as compared to men in this country.

The legal environment of America in the last third of the twentieth century has caused the reality of true equality under the law to be extended to juveniles and Selective Service registrants as well. The Gault case, which will be analyzed in detail later on in this book, buried forever the inhuman double standard under which constitutional rights were often taken away from juveniles charged with committing crimes.

Although it has been a slow, painful process, the United States Supreme Court is finally getting around to realizing that draft registrants are not cattle. Even though the American government clearly has the right to induct citizens without consulting them in order to protect all the people, still, at the same time, it must remember that registrants still are United States citizens with all the rights that go with this status.

Today there can be no doubt that the list of various types of United States citizens protected by our laws is still expanding from the original base of white male landowners. Two further areas come to mind in which rights for individuals have not caught up with those enjoyed by other groups. Prisoners and military personnel are such deprived groups. Although imprisonment demands many restrictions on the liberties and rights afforded to a prisoner, the penal aspects have received great emphasis. Today, the corrective process is receiving tardy but necessary attention. Any meaningful attempts to change attitudes of prisoners are doomed to failure if the conditions under which they live lack humanitarian safeguards unnecessarily. At least our society has come to the point where it is ashamed of the truth of the phrase "the state pen." Once treating prisoners like human beings is really believed in as assisting the correctional process, many of the harsh laws and procedures to which prisoners are subjected will be ended. Petitions of prisoners challenging various prison regulations recently have received sympathetic hearings in the courts. Still, areas exist in which the rights of prisoners need to be clarified. Recently many courts have thrown out strict regulations concerning prisoners sending and receiving mail. This is especially true when dealing with letters between a prisoner and his legal counsel. It is hard to see how censorship of the correspondence between attorneys and clients can be permitted. This is a clear violation of the privilege of secrecy in their relationship.

America's armed might is also feeling the tug of due process. Our country has progressed to a point where it no longer is satisfied with a blanket assurance that "this is an Army matter" when a serviceman gets in trouble. Far too many servicemen can furnish examples of instances in which the Military Code of Justice seemed far closer to being a Military Code of Injustice. Too often the accused was treated as if guilty and was not permitted the full protection of his rights which the Constitution guarantees to any criminal defendant. Granted that there is a unique necessity for discipline in the Armed Forces; yet this should not be extended to a point of the total loss of constitutional protection for the soldier involved. He is a United States citizen. Recognition of this fact has often been forgotten by the military. Today, it seems as if this state of affairs is fast changing. Given the horrid conditions in military prisons, the public feels that all safeguards must be followed to put only those who deserve this sort of fate in such a prison. Changes have been slow, but are progressing in this area as well.

The present-day concern that American citizens who happen to be soldiers as well, are ill treated by military justice has caused the United States Supreme Court to limit the authority of military courts when the same offense can also be prosecuted in a civilian court. No longer does the military have authority to try a soldier for a crime that was committed while the serviceman was on nonmilitary property in civilian clothes. Similarly, the military can no longer try a man for the same offense for which he has been tried previously in a civilian court. In the past, the military claimed the right to try the serviceman again on the theory that he has disgraced the military and violated their code since he is a serviceman twenty-four hours a day. The military tried these servicemen and if they were found guilty, they were imprisoned regardless of the fact whether they had been found innocent or guilty (and even served a sentence) in a civilian court. This has been held by the United States Supreme Court to be a violation of the constitutional protection against "double jeopardy." "Double jeopardy" means that a person cannot be tried twice for the same crime. One other recent protection guaranteed to servicemen is the right to select an attorney, whether civilian or military, to defend him. In the past, it was often made very hard for the serviceman to select an advocate other than from a list of officers that was submitted to him. These officers did not have to be attorneys and many times no attorneys were on the list.

The beginnings of our Constitution

It is within this climate of real concern for the rights of all citizens and all groups of citizens that we begin our examination of the constitutional system of the United States and the relation of the courts to this system. Unless we have some understanding of our Constitution, we will have a weak base upon which to build our knowledge in a variety of more specific areas of Urban Law. Just as 2,000 years ago all roads led to Rome, today all our legal situations lead to the United States Constitution.

The American Constitution is a unique document. Nothing like it existed at the time of its composition. This is not to say that John Adams and the other men who were responsible for writing it, pulled our Constitution out of thin air. They did not. As landed gentlemen who had received a considerable amount of schooling, the authors had been exposed to the classical tradition. The governmental forms that had been employed by Greece, Rome, Egypt, and the Holy Roman Empire, to name but a few of the great civilizations, were known to them. Before the Revolution, they were all citizens of the British Empire. The form of government employed by this empire was well known to them and influenced their own thinking greatly. The writers of our Constitution recognized the theoretical validity of the British approach, but quarrelled with the acts of the officials who carried out this policy in the colonies.

Examples of the harshness of British justice in the colonies are numerous. The fact that the citizens of Britain were allowed to pay lower taxes than the colonists were forced to pay is clear proof that true British protection under the law did not cross the Atlantic Ocean. In fact, the status of the colonies was so low that a British citizen who was charged with committing a crime in any one of the American colonies had the option of having his trial transferred to Britain. This would be roughly the same as allowing a white New Yorker in 1950 who killed a Harlem black man to choose a trial in the courts of New York or Mississippi. It is clear that Britain's pre-Revolutionary War treatment of the American colonies was a serious misuse of a legal system that had much to offer, especially in the relationship of the criminal defendant with the state.

The framers of the United States Constitution had two American models to draw upon in addition to the written version of the British legal system. First, there were the colonial constitutions of the thirteen colonies; secondly, there were the

Articles of Confederation. Both were too narrow and needed great additions in order to stand as a satisfactory model for a national government. Immediately after the Revolutionary War, it was hoped that the Articles of Confederation which were our first attempt at writing a national constitution, would work. This did not prove to be the case because these Articles were too loosely drawn and disjointed. The Articles left entirely too much power to each separate state. A real danger existed that the hard-won freedom achieved by the colonists at the cost of so much bloodshed would slip away. If America broke down into thirteen separate, tiny countries as it gave every indication of doing, it would be an easy task for England to reconquer its former territory. Once the new states started raising individual armies and charged rates for trade between individual states, the road to separate countries became very clear. It seemed to be inevitable that Britain, when it had temporarily cleared its board of trouble on the Continent and in its still remaining colonies, would pay a return visit to our shores. It was safe to presume also that the visitor would not come back as a beloved relative who had moved away. It was imperative that the new states unite.

It was within this framework of necessity and past failure that John Adams and his companions began their two-year job of writing our Constitution. The task must have been monumental. The first blush of success occasioned by ousting England had passed. More than a half dozen years of suspicion, arguing, and ill will between the states had followed in its wake. In many ways, it was necessary to start again at the beginning. America was blessed with great men at that time. George Washington was far more than a symbol and in many ways more resembled a colonial messiah. Alexander Hamilton, Thomas Jefferson, Arthur Gallitan, Benjamin Franklin, and others were all men of remarkable ability. It must be remembered that in those days America did not lose its truly great brains to industry and the financial world as it does today. Each and every great intellectual in America was at the disposal of the new government. Through it all and towering above all others in intelligence was Thomas Jefferson. No recounting of Jefferson's intellectual ability could be an exaggeration. During his presidency, John F. Kennedy assembled for a dinner some of the top American intellectuals. Kennedy observed to the assembled gathering that this was undoubtedly the greatest collection of brain power assembled at the White House since Thomas Jefferson dined there alone. Given the 165 years in between, this was the ultimate compliment.

Nowhere more than in the Constitution does the brilliance of our "Founding Fathers" remain for all succeeding generations to see and admire. Close on to two centuries later, their creation stands almost totally unchanged and is functioning quite smoothly. This in a country seventy times larger than it was in 1789.

In our Constitution was incorporated the desire of the states to be separate from each other while at the same time preserving and increasing national union. In a very different and more sophisticated way the complexities of present-day life have made even more urgent the need for a national government. Even in the early days, the sad lesson of division under the Articles of Confederation emphasized the need for a national government that would be at the same time both the slave and the master of the states. The unique solution of "preemption" solved this dilemma. It is necessary that we understand "preemption."

"Preemption" grants to the national government the authority to keep total control of certain powers *exclusively to itself*. The opposite to this is that the various states possess governing powers in those areas in which their powers have not been taken away by the federal government. In general, the federal government is supreme in dealings involving two or more states and also with the individual American citizen's relationship to these dealings between two or more states. There are many examples of this, such as: the defense of our country; interstate transportation of mail; health problems with national significance; radio and television programs beamed into many states; and many others. Over the last 180 years the role of the federal government has grown fantastically. So many areas touch the citizens of two or more states today that the situation has reversed itself totally since 1789. When this nation began, there was the fear that the superiority of the states would break us into thirteen separate countries. Today, there is the fear that the power of the federal government is so strong that the states will be reduced to the status of a harmless curiosity. This very real possibility must be blocked. Total federal superiority was not intended in our constitutional system and would have deep-seated disastrous consequences. Although there are many problems with his suggestion, President Nixon seems to have a good idea when he proposes to give back large amounts of federal funds to the states and cities. Maybe he shouldn't collect this money in the first place.

Checks and balances

The complex structure of our federal government system is caused by our basic three-part structure consisting of Legislative, Executive, and Judicial branches. The strength of this system is found in the series of checks and balances that prevents any one branch from drawing all the power to itself and thereby reducing the other branches to a less powerful position. This wrongful assumption of power by one branch or another has been the stumbling block that has prevented the governmental structure of other countries from ever becoming a real democracy. Although the spotlight concentrates on the function and fame of the Executive Branch more than on the Legislative or Judicial in our country, the system of "checks and balances" preserves essential equality. One reason for the seeming leading position of the presidency is that it is much easier to focus on the action of one man as contrasted with the action of a nine-man Judiciary or a 535-man (House and Senate) group. However, the president cannot do it alone. Harry S. Truman had a terrible two years from 1946 to 1948 when a Senate possessing a large Republican majority tied up the legislative process and passed few of the measures that President Truman desired. In a similar manner, Franklin D. Roosevelt's socialistic legislative efforts to end the great American depression of the 1930s were cut off at the roots by the United States Supreme Court decisions holding that most of this legislation violated the United States Constitution. The practical reality that the Executive cannot ignore the Legislative and Judicial and go it alone should not be discounted or forgotten.

Before passing on to a discussion of the powers and limitations of each of the three branches of the federal government, it is well for us to reflect for a minute on the truth of the saying that the United States is a nation under law. This must be done since the makeup and force of both our government and the liberty of our people come from this fact. Our system of laws carries with it a slavish following of clearly spelled-out methods of action. This fact is particularly clear in our Constitution. It is this following of set methods of action that has made us different in a fundamental manner from other countries. We do not have methods for revolution or constitutional suspension or procedures for shutting down our Legislature. More than other nations, we affirm the power of our Constitution as written and attempt to follow it in all our statutes and procedures. The great importance of our Constitution has enabled America to achieve internal stability of a unique nature.

Although most publicity concerning our government is centered around the office of the implementor, the president, the true starting point should be Capitol Hill. This is entirely in keeping with our statement that America is a nation under law. What better place for us to begin than the place where law begins? There is no need to turn this into a high-school civics class, complete with the cute drawings of a bill proposed by a senator or representative and follow its progress through committee hearings, the voting process of the House and Senate, conference committees, presidential passage or veto, resubmission, and so on. The details are beyond our grasp or our needs. However, we should keep in mind the complexity of the procedure and the number of people, both expert in the particular area and not, who must pass judgment upon a bill before the eventual day that it reaches the president's desk hopefully for signature. Many times the final product is in such a different form from the time when it was suggested by the originator that even he would have a hard time in recognizing his brain child. This may seem improper or even cruel, but it is not. The close inspection that a bill undergoes permits the striking out of weak points and the further emphasis of strong points in a proposal. In addition, the time needed for a bill to achieve passage allows time for the citizens whom the various members of Congress represent to be heard on the measure. Therefore, when bills become laws, they have been given a great deal of study and hopefully have been molded into the best possible shape. It would be silly to suggest that all bills that come out of Congress are perfect when they reach their final form. Obviously, we know that this is not the case. Politics often play too large a role in the final decision. In addition, it is quite true that some of the best legislation is the least appreciated by the public. This occurs especially in the case of complicated legislation in fields such as education and taxation.

Granted that the bills passed by Congress could be better (as could be anything done by mankind); it must be admitted that given the enormous problems of present-day living, Congress does an extremely good job. One reason for this is due to the "answerability" feature. "Answerability" is a nice way of saying: "What have you done for me lately, pal?" Each representative is called to account by the voters in his district every other year. Each senator is called to account every six years. If the voters are not happy with the quality of the work done by their elected officials, they have the opportunity to give them the gate and try their luck with another group of men. Since the office of a member of Congress is well paid and carries with it some fame, it is the rare man who does not desire to be reelected. More than anything else, it is the power of the voters in his district to oust him from office that forces all members of Congress to tow the line. If the people in the district do not participate by selecting and voting for candidates favorable to them, it is their own fault if a congressman or senator they do not like remains in office.

Both the Executive Branch through the president and the Supreme Court itself have the power to check the Legislature as effectively, if not as directly, as do the voters. The president can veto legislation that he does not think will be good for the country. If he does so, a two-thirds majority in each House is necessary to overturn the veto. The Supreme Court can also exercise a restraining hand upon the Congress. If a law is challenged and its opponents can convince the Supreme Court to consider their petition, the Court can in effect repeal the bill by declaring it to be unconstitutional. This will negate the work of the Congress and necessitate a new start with a new bill. The old bill which had become a law is now dead.

Although we rarely think of it as being so, the president does not have a totally free hand in his position. He must answer to all American voters each four years. With the addition of television, each presidential candidate is exposed to a degree of inspection unequaled in American history. Every speech, every decision, every appointment, and every part of his character and personality are up for consideration at all times. In addition, Congress can effectively hamstring a president by refusing to pass the legislation necessary to run the government properly. This becomes especially important when the bill deals with money appropriations. Nothing can grind the Executive wheels to a halt quicker than a lack of funds. Actually, the Congress has the Executive Branch coming and going. The income tax legislation must be passed by Congress. This means that Congress sets the amount of money that can be collected from citizens. In addition, Congress must pass the bills funding the specific programs which the Executive is charged with carrying out. All the cabinet areas such as Defense, State, Justice, Agriculture, Welfare; all the administrative agencies such as the Civil Service System, the Interstate Commerce Commision, N.A.S.A., etc., are dependent upon the Congress to set how much money they can receive for the next year. Although the Judicial does not have a direct check on the Executive, it can declare unconstitutional measures that the president has persuaded Congress to pass. In addition, it can rule against the government in lawsuits in which the United States is concerned directly.

The Supreme Court is not directly responsible to the voters because appointment to it is for life, but the members owe their appointment to the nomination of the president and the confirmation of the Senate. Removal of Supreme Court justices can only be for high crimes and this removal requires an impeachment trial in the House of Representatives. As to a law which the Supreme Court strikes down as unconstitutional, Congress is always free to pass the law again in a new form that hopefully could get around the constitutional objections of the Supreme Court.

From these three branches of government, that were set up in our Constitution, all the workings of our national government came. In actuality, the balance-of-power concept becomes tangled in the incredible complexity of details surrounding any government action or function. A detached, overall view will show that even with all the tangles, the concept of checks and balances still is possible and reasonably successful today. On a less grand scale, the individual states maintain the same type of balance of power between the three branches of state government. In addition to obeying the state constitution of the individual state in question, it is necessary in a like manner for the individual state constitution to obey in its essentials the United States Constitution. This must be done for two reasons. First of all, each state has expressly agreed at the time of its admission to the Union to be bound by the United States Constitution. It would be a contradiction for a state to agree to obey the United States Constitution and then turn around and pass a totally inconsistent provision in its own state constitution, statutes, or case law. The second reason why the state constitution must be in basic agreement with the United States Constitution comes from the first reason. Each and every citizen of a particular state is also a citizen of the United States and entitled to all the guarantees and all the rights and privileges that go with his status as a United States citizen. It would be a contradiction to guarantee these citizens rights on a federal level and deny them the same rights on a state level.

The Bill of Rights

The main body of the United States Constitution is fortified by the first ten amendments which are known familiarly as the "Bill of Rights." It is through the Bill of Rights that the working parts of the federal government as contained in the text of the United States Constitution are applied and made meaningful to the states. Without the first ten amendments the concept of a federal government would not work since no matter how smoothly it functioned in the abstract, there would not be a method available to bring these federal rights to the citizen of a state. The Bill of Rights performs this role and makes sure that each state gives all American citizens all the rights which they receive from the federal Constitution just because they are United States citizens.

To praise the Bill of Rights in a nation filled with large amounts of poverty, strife, and unhappiness may seem to be wrong. However, the Bill of Rights is nothing more than a way to bring all the protections of the Constitution to the level of the individual; to call the Bill of Rights wrong is to call the Constitution wrong. However, for two reasons this is not so. First of all, no one has been able to propose a better system. The series of checks and balances, if properly applied, guarantees equality for all within a smooth framework. All substitutes give up either equality or a smooth framework. Secondly and most importantly, praising the Constitution and its stepson, the Bill of Rights, is not a contradiction because we too often lose sight of the fact that the Constitution itself and the men applying it are not the same thing. This is an important fact. When criticizing the laws of this country, it is well to separate the Constitution as written and as applied. If, as is usually so, it is in the hearts and actions of individuals that the problem lies, it is wrong to condemn the Constitution. In this situation, the solution is not to change the law, but to change the attitudes of the persons applying the law. If we can't change the attitudes of these people, it is necessary to take the drastic step of removing them from authority and substitute for them persons who will apply the law as written.

For one hundred years our Constitution has guaranteed equal rights to blacks. Still we have not reached the point where this theoretical equality has been achieved in actuality. Who is to blame? It is clearly both those who administer the law and the voters that put them in office and encouraged them to misuse their powers. Only an aroused electorate both black and white can change this situation. In the seventies, it will be the concerned peaceful electorate, both black and white, who will succeed in this venture. Only then will the theoretical constitutional guarantees come into reality. When this is done, the administrators of the law will reach the state of perfection that our written law achieved a long time ago. This should not be laughed off as totally unrealistic. It honestly cannot be argued any longer that the whites do not want equality for the blacks. This in itself is a great step forward. In the past, it is questionable whether this desire for equality truly was present in a large number of whites.

The Bill of Rights is deceptively simple when read in an unsuspecting manner. The various promises are harder to put into practice than one would suspect. To give an example, the courts have written volumes of opinions on the one word "unreasonable" in the Fourth Amendment. In the abstract it is all well and good to assert that the Constitution prohibits "unreasonable searches and seizures," but to try to decide what is or is not reasonable in a particular fact pattern can be very difficult. Similar difficulties exist with virtually each amendment. Circumstances almost invariably exist that bring into question whether the constitutional guarantee actually was violated in the particular instance under inspection.

Another problem with interpreting individual rights is that they do not extend onward indefinitely in a vacuum. It is inevitable that instances will occur in which it is necessary to limit a constitutional guarantee in relative fashion because two different guarantees cross. The First Amendment guarantees of freedom of religion and separation of church and state are a perfect example of this. To avoid any confusion it is well to note that these clauses are sometimes referred to, respectively, as the "free exercise clause" and the "establishment clause." The employment of chaplains in the Armed Forces of the United States is a perfect example of choosing the "free exercise clause" over the "establishment clause" when dealing with a particular factual situation. Each branch of the service is aware of the need and right of their personnel to worship in the way that they choose. Yet, they often are on duty in places and at times in which it is not possible for them to attend services of their faith. For this reason, chaplains are hired by the Armed Forces even though it is at least arguable a violation of the "establishment clause" that holds that state (actually the First Amendment says "Congress," but its application is far broader than that) and church should be as separate as possible and that the state should not in any way become involved in religious matters. This is an example of balancing constitutional guarantees in the best interest of all, and the treating of constitutional guarantees as relative and not as absolute in nature. This is the only manner in which harmony between conflicting rights can be achieved.

In the matter of prayers in schools, the same two clauses cross again. This time the "establishment clause" is victorious. As to the matter of praying in school, there is not the urgency that is present in the case of Armed Forces personnel. School children still have sufficient opportunity outside of school to exercise their freedom of worship, whereas a soldier may not. For this reason the courts have emphasized the separation of church and state in the classroom situation and consequently have made it more important than the ability of a child to exercise his "freedom to worship" while in school.

Relativism (that is, picking and choosing between two different constitutional guarantees) in constitutional interpretation should be kept in mind. It is for this reason that the "freedom to assemble," for example, is limited by the qualification that it cannot be used to justify a riot or a treasonous group. Clearly the right of society in general to safety would be more important than the right of the people peaceably to assemble to plan to blow up the White House. In the area of "freedom of speech" the public's strong right to be spared from exposure to total filth and obscenity is more important than the total right to say or write anything, although some superliberals are not persuaded that this should be so.

In the first chapter of this book it was mentioned that there was a danger of making the concept of Urban Law so wide that its possible impact would be watered down greatly. One area in which this easily could happen is in a discussion of constitutional rights. Abstract discussions on such items as the limits to "freedom of association" are far from the most pressing problem that the urban poor must face. Still, it is permissible to use this discussion to demonstrate the import of relativism in constitutional interpretation. This fact will be demonstrated more clearly in later chapters, especially when the area of criminal statutes is under discussion. Except for death and taxes, there are exceptions to everything else in this world. We must remember this when talking about laws.

Summing up

When a man says, "I am an American," he is telling us a lot more than the mere fact that he lives in that part of the world called the United States. He is also saying he has the right to assemble where he wants and with whom he wants; and to do the same for his right to worship and his right to free speech and his right to be protected from unreasonable search and seizures and his right to vote no matter the color of his skin, and a whole large group of other rights. The total could never be matched in another country. In addition, he is a citizen of a three-sectioned national and state government that brings a degree of equality and stability that also can't be matched anywhere else in the world. Because of the power and majesty of our Constitution, we can talk about an Urban Law. Our Constitution is the backstop from which Urban Law and all other branches of law draw their power. Now that we have outlined the foundation, it is time to look at the various types of problems in the city and to see how Urban Law goes about trying to solve them.

Chapter 4

"Perry Mason" and His Pals

Setting the scene

A character in a play by William Shakespeare once suggested that the first thing his group should do when they reached power was to kill all the lawyers. A number of people still feel this way. Some have reason to think so, but most do not and even those who do have cause to dislike lawyers, must admit that a good one can be a great help.

If everyone in the neighborhood got sick, money would be pooled to get enough together to hire a doctor to cure the disease. Well, poverty and injustice are diseases which proper use of laws can go a long way toward curing. The experts in the legal fields are the ones to call upon. If they are not available in sufficient numbers presently, we must insist that the government hire more, on the one hand, and that lawyers presently in other fields devote some of their time to this field as well.

However, just as a doctor can't cure a disease until he is told what is wrong by the patient, lawyers can't help to end inequality and poverty unless the urban poor advise them and help them to realize where the greatest injustices lie. For the urban poor to do this, they must understand what

45

lawyers can and cannot do to help them. We shall try to do this in the present chapter because it is with the help of lawyers more than in any other way that the constitutional guarantees discussed in the last chapter can be made a reality enjoyed by all American citizens.

"Perry Mason" mysteries have sold more than fifty million copies in the United States over the years. Also, these stories written by Earl Stanley Gardner have been translated into over forty different languages and the "Perry Mason" television program ran for nine years in the United States on a first-run basis and is still running all over the world, in reruns. So it is fair to say that "Perry Mason" stories have been seen or read by hundreds of millions of persons in virtually every part of the world.

Real-life courtrooms, as opposed to the fictional ones in "Perry Mason," are not pretty places. Most are old, dirty, ill lighted, and overcrowded. Lawyers, court personnel, defendants, and other interested parties mill around waiting for their case to be called. Justice is handed down in an atmosphere of organized confusion. Somehow or other, the job gets done. The fact that the job gets done is proof of the dedication and ability of everyone involved. Crimes and lawsuits multiply, but government money to enable the court system to keep pace lags far behind. Yet, through it all, somehow or other the system functions in a manner that guarantees that justice will, for the most part, be served.

The lack of smoothness in our court system must be recognized. Inefficiency occurs often. The system is too overworked to afford the luxury of many dramatic, prolonged "Perry Mason" type legal chess games. Only for dramatic effect in a book, television series, or movie can the "Perry Mason" type performance occur with any regularity; and only in Earl Stanley Gardner does the defense attorney always win.

Though "Perry Mason" is unrealistic, he is important. Far too often, Americans (to say nothing of those in other countries) picture our legal system through their exposure to "Perry Mason." When they encounter the real thing, a great shock occurs. Often they are then forced to revise their ideas of

American courts and American justice in general. Just imagine if every American lawyer were "Perry Mason"! Each courtroom in this country would be filled with a series of dramatic, flamboyant cases, while ten others just as flamboyant and dramatic would be ready to roll when the ones before them ended. The "nuts and bolts" type case would never be covered. Clearly the "Perry Mason" type system will not work. Let us see what type system does work.

The above discussion serves well to introduce our discussion of the role of the lawyer. The very name "lawyer" indicates that one in this profession spends his life engaged in dealing with law. As we have seen in our overcrowded society, law is composed of far more than courtroom appearances alone. It deals also, in an intimate manner, with the business and personal transactions that a man uses as a substitute for a courtroom answer to his problems. Therefore, like our legal system itself, a lawyer's occupation has two parts: courtroom appearances and legal substitutes in place of courtroom appearances. In other words, a lawyer must be both an advocate and a counselor. To return for a moment to what we said in Chapter 2, the lawyer is involved with both the second and the third definitions of law. As an advocate, the lawyer deals with the application of statutes and cases in a courtroom in order to arrive at a decision in a particular legal controversy. As a counselor, the attorney is much closer to our third definition of law: the legal environment. This is true since as a counselor, though he must take note of statutes and cases to advise his client, he uses them only to guide the client's day-to-day business affairs in such a way that he won't have to use the courts.

No attempt to understand the role of an attorney has any hope of success unless the distinction between the attorney as advocate and the attorney as counselor is kept clearly in mind. Much of the confusion and criticism surrounding lawyers is due to the fact that the public does not understand this difference. How can one know if an attorney is acting properly if he does not know what an attorney is supposed to do? Lawyers are to blame for this confusion. They have not explained their function properly to the public. Unless they do so, it is not fair to expect the public to appreciate what they are doing.

The attorney as counselor

In a courtroom, the function of an attorney is easy to understand. He is trying to persuade the judge or jury that his client should win. However, when the attorney acts as counselor, his function is not so clear at first glance. In no other profession is the goal of the man whose services are hired as unclear as those of a lawyer acting as a counselor. A doctor holds himself out as being able to heal the sick. An accountant promises to give a client an accurate dollar-and-cents picture of his financial holdings. A social worker promises to make known to the client all the public and private agency resources available to aid a client. But what does the lawyer as counselor do?

The word "counselor" itself tells us everything and nothing concerning this function of an attorney. A counselor gives counsel. This means that he listens to a problem or proposed activity as presented, and usually after proper research and interpretation of the statutes and cases already decided on this problem, he informs the client of the legal implications of the problem or proposed activity. This legal counselling service for which the attorney expects to be paid adequately marks this part of an attorney's role as one of being an information bank for hire. Since the law has penalties which exist to guarantee that what it says is followed, the client knows that his actions and problems are important. The lawyer, as counselor, has the obligation to spell out all the possible outcomes from a legal point of view.

From birth to death, there are legal implications to practically every action we take. The state wishes to insure that babies are going to be cared for when they leave the hospital. For this reason, there are laws demanding parents fill out birth records. The state wants to make sure that its future citizens will be able to carry on the functions of government and society. For this reason, there are laws that make attendance at school obligatory. The state wishes that all people have equal treatment under the laws. For this reason, the United States Constitution was adopted and other laws have been passed. The state wishes the people to be safe from attacks against their person and property. For this reason, criminal laws have been enacted and enforced. Finally, the state wishes that all people who live in this country receive proper burial. So it has legislated to provide for burials at state expense when necessary. This very brief life-to-death listing of laws has omitted thousands and thousands of areas in which laws have been passed to regulate conduct.

All laws are a recognition that people cannot live together, in harmony, without regulation. In a world teeming with people, nearly every act one person performs has an effect on some other person or persons. If one man steals, he obtains money unjustly and the victim loses it unjustly. If two competitive companies fix prices, consumers have to pay more unjustly. Any dealings with the public, of any nature, have an effect upon others. This effect on other people gives the state, who after all represents all the people, an interest in the matter. This state interest is what we mean by "legal implications." It is in this area of forecasting legal implications that the lawyer holds himself out as being an expert. He is able to tell the client what legal effects follow under a given set of circumstances. In many cases, the lawyer can go so far as to take the proper legal steps for his clients in order to bring about the proper legal implications on behalf of the client. This is merely an extension of the attorney's role of giving advice as to the legal implications of contemplated conduct. As a counselor, a lawyer is a forecaster, a resource man, and an advisor. He retains a separate identity from the client. Once the lawyer spells out all the legal implications of the client's proposed action, it is up to the client to decide if he wishes to perform the act or not. If the legal implications of the proposed action are such as to make the action unwise or unappealing to the client, a proposed new course of action with its own set of legal implications can be examined by the lawyer and client as an alternative to the original plan.

The attorney as advocate

As an advocate in a court case, the lawyer is a totally different person than the lawyer as a counselor. The change is almost schizophrenic. As an advocate, the lawyer becomes the client. Once a client has engaged the services of an attorney for a courtroom appearance, all the actions in the case for the client are performed by the attorney. The client speaks through his attorney who is his advocate, and the court will listen only to the attorney and ignore anything said by the client unless the attorney calls his client to the stand as a party. Of course, the Constitution permits every man to be his own attorney; but once the party decides to employ a lawyer to speak for him in court, he has surrendered the right to speak for himself. Only a lawyer who has been admitted to the practice of law in the state in question is granted this great privilege of being recognized by the court as being, in effect, the client. The client cannot select a nonlawyer to speak for him and have this man recognized as representing the client.

Caryl Chessman was mentioned in the last chapter as a victim of California, Section 209, although it must be emphasized that the Section 209 violation for which he was executed was entirely independent from his crimes with David Knowles. Chessman is also famous in California law for his attempts to defend himself during his Section 209 trial. Chessman, although poorly educated, was very shrewd. His deep study of California criminal law and procedure made him an expert of this subject. Few, if any lawyers, knew as much about the California criminal law as Chessman. Of course, Chessman had his life riding on the outcome. This would make quite a difference. Also, while being locked in a cell, there was little else that he could do with his idle hours except study and scheme. However, the reasons for his great knowledge of California Criminal Law are immaterial. Chessman could and did defend himself, most of the time with great skill.

Three of the most controversial decisions by the judge in the trial revolved around Chessman's desire to defend himself. The first point is clearer than the other two. Chessman wanted to cross-examine the witnesses himself, while he was still being defended by a court-appointed attorney. Naturally, the judge refused this request, as we would expect from our previous discussion of this point. After Chessman fired his attorney and began to conduct his own defense, he wanted to be able to do everything in court that an attorney could do; and he also desired permission to visit law libraries outside the prison walls in order to do research on the legal questions involved in preparing his defense. The trial judge refused both of these requests. After much deliberation, the California Supreme Court upheld the lower court on the theory that, although a defendant had every right to defend himself, he was not an attorney-at-law and thus not entitled to the extra privileges reserved exclusively for attorneys. The wisdom of this decision is questionable, especially in a case in which a man's life was at stake. "Equal protection" would seem to demand that as much as possible, a defendant who chooses to present his case himself should be treated as if he were an attorney. The Chessman incident was not introduced here to consider this point. The only importance this controversy has for us is as an illustration of the situation in which the distinction between the client representing himself and the client hiring an attorney, as his advocate in court, was of vital importance.

When the lawyer dons his fighting togs as an advocate, a wholly different set of duties, privileges, and standards surrounds him than when he was acting as a counselor. The aloof status of an outsider hired to give advice on legal implications is gone. He ceases to be merely a hired hand. In a very real sense, the attorney as advocate becomes his client. The advocate speaks for his client in court and to a very large extent thinks for his client as well. About the only thing that the advocate does not do is to go to jail or pay the fine for the client if he loses. With the possible exception of a surgeon, there is no other professional man entrusted with the same degree of responsibility by the client. The legal profession must take great care to fulfill this duty in a worthy manner.

Why do advocates have the power to assume the role of the client? When we stop to consider it, this is a truly remarkable privilege. For the purposes of a trial, the client who employs an attorney ceases to exist, unless his attorney calls his client to the stand as a party. It is as if the client has vanished into thin air. Of course, a wag will answer that it is the attorney who does the vanishing act when it is time to serve the sentence. No doubt, this is true. However, until the time of reckoning, it is the attorney who assumes the task of explaining and justifying the actions of the defendant.

The justification of this unique role for an advocate is derived from the United States Constitution, and more specifically from the Bill of Rights (the first ten amendments to the United States Constitution). History tells us that examples of the privileged status of an advocate can be found in the earliest origins of English government, and even in such earlier civilizations as the Greek, Roman, Assyrian, and Charlemagnian, to name but a few. The final result of these earlier concepts of an advocate and his function can be found best in the United States Constitution because our country is so interested in bringing equality under the law to all our citizens.

The American boast of equality to all under the law would be an empty boast if proper procedures were not established to insure that equality truly exists. When speaking about the individual's protection under our system of laws, we are in large measure talking about the Bill of Rights. This is especially true in regard to criminal trials. It is easy for Americans to take for granted such constitutional guarantees in criminal cases as the right to confront witnesses; the right to trial by jury; the right to a speedy trial; freedom from unreasonable search and seizure; and the right of an accused to have the assistance of counsel. Unless a system of government actually guarantees and enforces these protections for its citizens in all circumstances, the boast of equality under law is a farce and a mockery.

Guarantees of equality are nothing but a hollow shell if the benefits do not reach all the people. One constitutional guarantee of note is the requirement that all accused must be tried on specific charges. This is to prevent the railroading of citizens by charging them with a vague offense like being a "bad person." Along with the constitutional obligation to specifically name the statutory violation with which the defendant is charged, there is also the obligation for the government to *prove* these charges beyond a reasonable doubt. Without benefit of legal counsel, in most cases there would be the real possibility that the accused person was convicted because he lacked the legal capability to raise the reasonable doubt and not because a reasonable doubt, in the legal sense, did not in fact exist. As in all sciences, method is most important in the law. Often, *how* you say something is just as important as *what* you say. A lawyer is a guarantee that what is said will be said in the manner most favorable to his client.

In our legal system, the question to be decided is whether the government in a criminal case can prove beyond a reasonable doubt that the defendant committed the crime with which he is charged. This should be the only question. "Equal protection" for all is lost if the added question as to whether the defendant actually was mentally and emotionally capable of presenting his side of the case must be asked as well. Since the various states set very strict standards with which a would-be attorney must comply before he is admitted to the practice of the law, a guarantee exists that the client's case will be presented in a proper manner. The role substitution performed by an attorney acting as an advocate is the best possible way of assuming that only the merits of the case will be in issue. The licensing of attorneys is a procedure which guarantees that the substitute for the defendant will be legally capable of presenting his client's case in as favorable a light as possible. Granted that some lawyers are more able than others; this system is still the best way of assuring that at the very least every person's case can be presented competently, if not brilliantly.

Unless the advocate becomes the client, the intellectual inequality between parties that would destroy "equal protection" could easily occur. Some Americans, often through no fault of their own, would not be capable of presenting their own case even with expert advice. It is necessary that the advocate become the client. This leads to the perpetual question: "How can you defend someone whom you know to be guilty?" The answer is that judging whether the client is guilty is none of the advocate's business. This is the function of the judge or the jury. Of course, the advocate should try to obtain the truth from his client; but short of helping the client to invent a clever lie, he must work with the story that the client gives him. We must keep in mind that it is the burden of the government to prove the defendant guilty. There is no obligation on the part of the defendant to say so himself. In fact, the United States Constitution guarantees the defendant this protection. To this constitutional guarantee should be added the Sixth Amendment protection of right to counsel. Putting these constitutional guarantees together, the sum total is that the advocate has the right to present his client's case in such a way that the government must overcome it and prove the opposite beyond a reasonable doubt. All attorneys, in whatever capacity they are acting, are officers of the court. This restricts their conduct to actions which aid the cause of justice. This would prevent an attorney from knowingly lying for his client or manufacturing false evidence. Short of this, the attorney as advocate has a free hand in defending his client.

As pointed out, there are great differences between the attorney's role as a counselor and as an advocate. It would not be wise to allow the counselor to act as the client. The business world, which operates on a delicate balance with supply and demand as its key, would become hopelessly bogged down if every business transaction were as vigorously protected as a man's constitutional rights are protected. It is neither necessary nor practical to do so. Clearly, there are differences in the lawyer's authority between his role as counselor and his role as advocate. In fact, there are even differences within his role as advocate depending upon whether the lawyer is an advocate in a civil or criminal case. In a civil case, both the attorney and the client are more restricted than they would be in a criminal case since it is an action of one private party against another, and not all the people (the government) against one private party.

The responsibilities of all attorneys

The responsibilities of attorneys, whether they are acting as counselors or advocates, are quite strict. As "officers of the court," they are charged with aiding the administration of justice. All the attorney's actions, advice, and research must have as the main goal the increase of justice in our country. Upon admission to the practice of law in a state, the beginning attorney promises to devote all his efforts to the upholding of justice. Every action of his from then on possessing any conceivable sort of legal implication will be measured and examined. If the action of the attorney does not come up to the standard established for aiding justice, the lawyer involved can and should be punished. More than anyone else, the lawyer knows the law and in most instances has profited financially from his knowledge of the law and the privilege of applying this knowledge to make a good living for himself and his family. Therefore, if the attorney strays from the standard set for the proper administration of justice, he has no valid reason to expect mercy from the authorities.

As a further proof of the unique relationship between a lawyer and his client, a reference to the privilege of "confidentiality" should be made. Any private discussion between the lawyer and the client is secret and the lawyer is not free to mention it to anyone under any circumstances, without the permission of the client. This is a very serious obligation and binds the lawyer whether he be acting as a counselor or advocate. Of course the client is free to tell anyone what he said to the attorney, or what the attorney advised him, if he wishes. Few other types of relationships are as heavily protected: doctor-patient; clergyman and parishioner; and in a coule of states, licensed social worker and client. This added degree of freedom for the client brought about by "confidentiality" is a great help to both the client and the lawyer. The client is able to tell all the details of his actions without fear that the lawyer will tell someone else. The attorney receives more facts and has more to work with in arriving at a proper course of action. The only restriction on a lawyer is that he cannot falsify evidence or encourage the client to lie in court. "Confidentiality" is a key weapon in the arsenal of the attorney-client relationship, and it serves as proof of the great degree of approval that the law places on this relationship.

It is easy to condemn a lawyer for not observing his function as an "officer of the court" in aiding the administration of justice. Often the attorney is wrongfully condemned as acting against the interests of the smooth administration of justice. In fact, he is often acting in the best interests of the administration of justice, but those who criticize him have an incorrect idea concerning the dimensions of his obligation to assist in the administration of justice.

A layman often doesn't understand that an attorney is obligated to do his very best for his client even when it is clear that if the client were victorious, a mistake would be made. It is hard for many to accept the fact that the administration of justice can be served by an attorney who uses all of his skill, training, and eloquence to obtain a favorable verdict for an undeserving client. Rather than condemn an attorney for representing an undeserving client, he should be heartily congratulated. In our society, as we have said before, no man is adjudged as guilty simply because of the act of committing a crime. It is necessary in a criminal matter for the state to *prove* that he committed a crime. Unless the state can prove that a violation of the law occurred, the man is entitled to go free. In the same way, in a civil case it is necessary for the other side to prove that their arguments are more persuasive. When talking about the attorney as advocate, great care was taken to explain that because of the presence of an attorney the intelligence or legal savvy of the client was not that important. It is up to the state to prove beyond a reasonable doubt that the defendant committed the crime with which he was charged. The attorney as advocate is the best possible safeguard that the state has fulfilled its obligation to prove that the defendant was guilty. The lawyer possesses the intelligence and legal skill to nullify any serious inequality in this respect. This is the best way possible to narrow the controversy to the exact spot where it belongs, namely: Can the state prove beyond a reasonable doubt that the defendant committed the crime with which he is charged? Again, it should be repeated that everything said above concerning the role of an attorney in a criminal case applies with slightly less force in a civil case.

The obligation to prove guilt is one of the greatest safeguards for a free society. In an individual instance, it does not appear to be correct to permit a man to go free when every indication appears that he is guilty. However, unless the state is compelled to go one step farther and convert suspicions into proof, the possibility exists that the suspicions might be wrong. Once suspicions become more important than proof, equality under law is lost. Like many other evils, there is great temptation to begin tampering with the criminal burden of proof which demands that the charge be proved beyond a reasonable doubt. Numerous excuses for doing so come to mind readily. The unfortunate part is that the use of excuses quickly becomes a habit. Newspapers occasionally carry stories of mistakes in our justice system that lead to the wrongful conviction of a defendant. There is no question that this sort of tragic mistake occurs even when proof beyond a reasonable doubt is demanded. Lower these requirements and the number of people wrongly convicted of crimes will skyrocket. The attorney's role would be made ineffective. Abuses, influence peddling, bribery, and various other evils would occur frequently. American justice as we know it would be gone. The foundation supporting all our laws, statutes, courts, and agencies of government would disappear into thin air.

It is easy enough to talk glowingly in the abstract about the merits of a legal system that protects the defendant even to the point where everyone assumes he is guilty, but cannot prove that he is actually so. In the concrete, great restraint is necessary on the part of the government to permit a man who it is morally certain is guilty to walk out a free man because the technicalities of proof are lacking. Still, if this governmental restraint is not exercised, the foul odor of a true police state will begin to lurk in the air. In the short run, it is shocking to permit a crime to go unpunished; but in the long run, far more innocent people will be punished if the basis of "proof beyond a reasonable doubt" is abandoned. Even in the present system with its elaborate safeguard of appeals, mistakes are made. In a system with less safeguards, it stands to reason that the number of mistakes would rise.

Now that a fair trial for all has been discussed, the case of the alleged murderer or rapist or child molester can be looked at more fairly. It is in this area that many people tend to question whether a lawyer is aiding the administration of justice. It is hard for them to appreciate that the advocate who does battle on such a client's behalf is doing what he should. Even if the attorney for a thoroughly evil client defends him with the same nerve as was displayed by General Custer at the Little Big Horn River, he is to be congratulated and not condemned. As established, unless the only question is "can the state prove the facts beyond a reasonable doubt?" we are not operating within the democratic framework. Even when defending a rapist or murderer, all that the attorney does is to even the odds by removing the variables of lack of intelligence or legal sophistication from importance and thus insuring a more fair outcome. In no case more than in one concerning a person who is so demented as to murder, rape, or molest someone, is there more of a need to eliminate the variables and consider only the charge in question. Generally, the facts are so clear in such a case that even the best of trial attorneys would have little effect except to guarantee that the client's constitutional right to a fair trial has been protected totally.

So far the legal profession has emerged with a clean bill of health in this chapter. It is the belief of the author that for the most part this judgment is well merited. This chapter has attempted to explain the role of the attorney in great detail. Those who feel that they have been wronged by an attorney in the past would be well advised to review this belief in light of this chapter's discussion concerning the proper role of an attorney. This might reduce the large amount of dislike and mistrust of attorneys that exists.

Bad judges and bad lawyers

It does seem that one must in all honesty agree that the legal profession deserves a better reputation than it presently receives. However, only an ostrich with his head firmly stuck in the sand would be able to say that all judges and all lawyers perform their duties in a way that brings credit to the legal profession. Those who don't should be brought to task and made to do so, or, if necessary, be barred from continuing in the legal profession.

One of the great jewels of our legal system consists in the high standard of honesty and competence displayed by our judges. A small few do not live up to this high standard. If possible, these backsliders should be warned so that they will take the necessary steps themselves to conform to acceptable standards. If not, they should be removed. We must always be on our guard to see that this type of pressure is not politically motivated, but that it stems from true concern for maintaining the highest standards of justice.

Many states are establishing committees to see that individual citizens or groups of citizens have an opportunity to complain concerning the poor quality of the administration of justice by judges and other court employees in their area. The Massachusetts procedure is an excellent example of such a rule that attempts to protect the public. The Massachusetts procedure encourages all citizens and bar associations (groups of lawyers) to file their complaints with a special committee set up by the state for the sole purpose of investigating all complaints as to the honesty and fairness of judges and all other court personnel. This committee must investigate all complaints. The Supreme Judicial Court of the state has the final authority to reprimand, suspend, or remove the judge in question if it agrees with a bad report handed down by the complaint committee. If the offense was extremely serious, the judge could be disbarred. This would mean that he would be prevented as well from practicing law in any form. Finally, if it is believed that a crime was committed by the judge, the complaint could be referred to the grand jury for possible indictment and prosecution. Concerned groups of urban residents who feel they have a just complaint in this regard would be well to investigate and make use of procedures existing in their state to handle this problem. If procedures don't exist, they should demand their elected representatives pass laws to bring this type of check on the conduct of judges and other court personnel into existence.

In the same way, a client who has a complaint against an attorney should call this matter to the attention of the local bar association. They will be glad to hear of it because one poor lawyer can give all the good ones a bad name. In much the same manner as happens when there is a complaint against a judge, the case will be investigated and when appropriate, referred to the highest court of the state. This court has the power to publicly scold, suspend, disbar, or recommend grand jury action as the case may be, if it agrees that the attorney in question is guilty of misconduct. An alternate method of getting back losses caused by an unethical or incompetent attorney would be to sue for damages in a malpractice case. However, these rarely succeed because most lawyers are totally ethical and perform their tasks with ability. Usually the fault lies with the client who does not understand the proper function of an attorney and expects him to be a combination of "Perry Mason" and "Superman." Alas, a lawyer is a mere human like the rest.

Summing up

After reading this chapter, no one will have to be told that the author of this book is a lawyer. Also it is clear that he thinks lawyers do a very good job on the whole in helping those who seek their aid. The most encouraging fact is that the government is finally becoming aware of the real need for lawyers to help rid America of injustice and poverty. At the same time, more young lawyers than in the past are showing a real interest in entering this field. Oh, problems still exist. Politics, greedy big businessmen, and special interest groups have tried to limit the effectiveness of many of these programs. However, the 1960s have shown clearly that the government and its lawyers are willing to fight in the ghettos. It is up to the poor to welcome aid and direct these experts so that they will do the maximum amount of good for the urban poor.

CHAPTER 5

How Courtroom Wheels Turn

Setting the scene

In the last chapter we talked about the role for an attorney in our society and how important attorneys are for the day-to-day running of our country and how they can be of help to the poor. In this chapter, we will be examining our criminal court system in detail for three reasons. First, it will explain more in detail the role and need for attorneys in our society. Secondly, it will show again the concern that the American government has for the rights of all its citizens. Finally, it will give the citizen an idea as to the protection he receives if he is charged with a crime, while at the same time showing the great efforts that the government is making to rid the cities of crime so that the average, law-abiding citizen can earn his living in peace.

Legal aid for the poor

Although our legal system has always recognized the need to have an attorney represent a defendant in a criminal trial, it is surprising that until a few years ago a large group of defendants traditionally were deprived of the assistance of counsel in criminal trials. Of course, reference is being made to defendants who could not afford a lawyer. Until ten years ago most states did not provide and pay for attorneys to represent those who could not afford to hire an attorney except in cases where it was possible to sentence the defendant to lose his life (a capital case) if found guilty. Almost every state historically had made some arrangement for attorneys to represent all defendants charged with crimes that could carry the death penalty. This is understandable from a "due process" standpoint. Also there would be a real question of "cruel and unusual punishment" in violation of the Eighth Amendment if a man could go to his death if the assistance of counsel necessary to prevent this fate were denied because of an inability to afford an attorney.

Until ten years ago, the courts did not hold that the constitutional guarantee of "the right to assistance of counsel" extended to the point of any obligation on the part of the government to provide and pay for legal counsel for defendants not facing a possible death sentence who could not afford an attorney. If this defendant could obtain the services of an attorney, the court had to permit the attorney to conduct the defense for his client. However, if the defendant wanted but could not obtain an attorney, the court had no authority to obtain one for him. In most states, this defendant was treated as if he really did not want an attorney because he wanted to defend himself. The history of the ending of this extremely unjust situation is interesting as still another example of the legal environment shaping the application of the law.

Since the early 1930s, federal courts (as opposed to most state courts) had held that it would be a denial of equal treatment for all under the law to deny any defendant the access to an attorney in *any* criminal case merely because he couldn't afford one. The case that triggered this decision was the infamous "Scottsboro Boys" case (*Powell* v. *Alabama*) in which eleven blacks were sentenced to death for allegedly raping two tramp white girls in a railroad boxcar. The trial was filled with the type of prejudice that has given "Southern justice" a somewhat deserved black eye. To illustrate the questionability of these decisions, one of those convicted was blind and another was sexually defective. The judge in this case where the defendants' lives could be at stake, at one point refused their request to appoint an attorney for them since they had no funds and instead made all local attorneys responsible for representing them. As a reaction to the outrageous conduct of the judge in this case, the United States Supreme Court set down the rule binding in all criminal cases in federal courts and in all possible death sentence cases in any court, state or federal, that the court must appoint at government expense an attorney for any defendant without adequate funds who wished to be so defended. This was an addition to the constitutional right to counsel and a large step toward equality of the laws for all alike whether rich or poor.

The United States Supreme Court did not take the opportunity that the Scottsboro case (*Powell* v. *Alabama*) gave it to force all criminal courts in the nation to appoint and provide for payment for an attorney whenever a criminal defendant who could not afford an attorney wanted one. By passing up this opportunity in 1932, the Supreme Court in effect said to the states: "We are going to see that all defendants who cannot afford an attorney will be able to have one if they want in all criminal cases in our federal courts, but except for cases possibly carrying a death sentence, you do not have to do so if you do not decide it is necessary in your state."

This approach to the appointment of attorneys for defendants without funds remained as law for close to thirty years. In 1942, the Supreme Court looked at this question again and emphasized the ruling it had made on this matter in the *Powell* case. However, by 1960 the legal environment had caught up with this procedure and the need for a change was clear.

The direct cause for this change was provided in a strange, but heart-warming way. Earl Gideon, a pathetic little man, was the leading figure, Gideon, a habitual criminal, was arrested for breaking into a pool room in Florida. Incorrectly, Gideon insisted at his trial that the United States Constitution said he had a right to a lawyer. As we have seen, this was not totally true. The Constitution at that time preserved a "right to counsel" in a state court only if the defendant could pay for it or there was the possibility of a death sentence. Gideon did not fit in either category and the judge in the Florida state court properly refused to appoint an attorney to represent him under the Florida law then in effect.

Gideon was convicted and from his prison cell composed in ¸encil an appeal to the United States Supreme Court. It was this pencil-written petition filled as it was with misspellings, improper punctuation, and fifth-grade grammar mistakes that the United States Supreme Court chose as the case it would use to review its refusal to make court-appointed and paid attorneys available in all criminal courts and in all criminal cases whenever the defendant wanted, but could not hire an attorney. Abe Fortas, then a top Washington labor lawyer, was the court-appointed advocate for Gideon in front of the United States Supreme Court. He won and from that time on all states have been obligated to make the constitutional right to counsel in criminal cases truly effective by appointing at state expense an attorney to defend any criminal defendant who desired but couldn't afford an attorney in *any* criminal case.

It is heart-warming that such a radical shift in American legal procedure could be started in a prison cell by an uneducated drifter. It is safe to say that this could not happen in any other country. Nowhere else does the individual truly matter so much as in America. Being the character that Gideon was, once his right to a new trial had been won and counsel was to be appointed for him at his retrial, he attempted to refuse to have counsel appointed on the theory that if he could persuade the Supreme Court, he certainly could handle this case himself. He finally changed his mind and permitted a court-appointed attorney to defend him. It turned out to be a good thing for Gideon. Because of a lack of technical proof (rules Gideon never could have known himself), Gideon was found not guilty on his retrial. Undeserving as he is, American justice owes Earl Gideon a great deal.

Gideon freed American justice from one of its worse contradictions. The constitutional guarantee of right to legal representation was a hollow mockery if denied to those who could not afford a lawyer. In most cases, those who could not afford lawyers had more need of their services than anyone else. This is so since this presumably less-educated class of people would have a more difficult time in presenting a clear, penetrating analysis of the legal merits of their position than would a wealthier, better-educated defendant. For the law to say you can have counsel if you can afford one falls far short of the true equality for all under the law standard that guided the constitutional framers and subsequent judicial interpreters. By 1960, this fact had become clear to compassionate members of the legal profession. As a whole, lawyers supported and applauded the rationale of the *Gideon* case even though it has increased their work load greatly at fairly low rates of pay provided by the state.

Although the Constitution stops short of requiring the state to provide access to attorneys in civil cases, the philosophy behind *Gideon* motivated state legislatures, the United States Congress, and private foundations to take significant action in this area as well. The Johnson administration's "Great Society" concept had access to legal advice for all as one of its goals. The Legal Services Program, which was a part of the Office of Economic Opportunity, has tried to meet the need and has made a contribution in this area. Much is left to be done, but it is encouraging to see that attempts are being made to provide attorneys to assist all the poor in all of their legal problems.

Weaknesses in areas such as attorney pay, work load, investigatory services, and cooperation with court and social work agency personnel (especially in the area of the attorney-client privilege) hinder the effort to secure effective free legal assistance for all the poor in the truest sense of the Sixth Amendment guarantee of the "right to counsel." This should not hide the fact that the greatest handicap to making the "right to counsel" a reality, the client's lack of funds, has been removed. The rest of the problems are mere technicalities which large amounts of time, money, experience, and good judgment hopefully will solve. Lack of legal assistance for the poor was a fatal weakness and was cured none too soon. Some of the greatest injustices that occurred in the American legal system might have been avoided many years ago if lawyers had been made available free of charge to the poor.

In a thoroughly subjective way, Earl Gideon deserves a place in American legal history as far more than a mere legal reformer. Praise for Gideon must be tempered by the realization that he was motivated by self-interest in avoiding a prison stretch for a crime that he may not have committed, more than he was motivated by any burning desire to strike a blow for freedom and justice under the laws. Given his situation, this is understandable. However, the real importance of Gideon is that it is a showcase for the American legal system at its best. Even a semiliterate drifter locked up in a Florida prison was protected and assisted by American justice. If you are not suitably impressed by this fact, think for a minute. What chance do you suppose that a pencil-written complaint from any private citizen, let alone from a Florida convict, would have of reaching the desk of, for example, the president of one of our billion-dollar corporations? In a society in which wealth rules as king, a letter full of misspellings, incorrect punctuation, and poor grammar written by one unknown citizen would be a waste of time. If the writer were lucky and the secretary who read the complaint compassionate, he might receive a mimeograph form letter reply. A result such as Gideon received from the United States Supreme Court would be unthinkable in the corporate world or in the government of any other country for that matter. Only in America could the *Gideon* situation occur. One seeking comfort in these hectic days in which it is fashionable to heap scorn on our system of justice has to go no further than *Gideon*. This case is proof that American justice can work and it is a strong hope for our future. Of course, it would be wrong to use *Gideon* as an excuse to stop our efforts to obtain better types of free legal assistance for the poor. *Gideon* is an excellent start, but only just that: a start.

It does not speak well for the legal profession that the next subject must be discussed. However, since the rights of a client are involved in a crucial manner, it is necessary to do so. Although it is supposed to occur far more often than is actually true, it is undeniable that cases occur in which the counsel for a criminal defendant fails to protect the rights of his client adequately. Just as the "right to counsel" is a joke if it does not provide in an effective manner for those who wish but cannot afford an attorney, it is likewise a futile guarantee if the attorney for the defendant does not or cannot function on his client's behalf with the degree of competence guaranteed by the man's admission to and continuance of his practice of the law. The possible causes of ineffectiveness or inadequacy in attorneys are varied in nature. Senility, greed, laziness, distraction, overwork, and pride are some of the more common. The above catalogue appears more moral than legal in origin. This is so and for good reason. Failure to give the performance due for the fee accepted is a sin against justice as well as a rupture of the promised professional relationship. It is immaterial whether the attorney is paid by the client directly or by the state in a case in which the client cannot afford to do so. In either event, the attorney who fails to fulfill his obligation is at fault and should be censured in both the legal and the moral spheres.

The right to effective counsel demands adequate preparation by the defendant's attorney. If he is still applying knowledge learned in law school (as opposed to techniques) without the light of recent decisions even sullying his invincible ignorance of the present state of the law, it is pure luck if the attorney performs his task competently. No lawyer can keep all the changes in the various legal fields in his memory. Hard work is necessary to incorporate all the latest legal rulings and interpretations into the fact situation at hand. Brilliant insights developed at the sixth race at Belmont Park or on the golf course will not substitute. Only elbow grease will work.

If laziness on the part of the attorney is the largest reason for ineffectiveness, curiously, overwork is the seond greatest reason for ineffectiveness; it might even be first. Although no less to be condemned, it is more understandable. There are only so many working hours in the day. Many civil cases demand great research into laws and regulations especially in the tax area. Complicated paperwork can reduce drastically the time that an attorney has to prepare his criminal cases. The same situation occurs if the attorney takes on too many criminal cases. With rare exception, it is of little importance how fast a talker an attorney is. If he has not done his homework, he will fail.

These warnings about advocates doing less than an acceptable job for their clients should not be interpreted as an indication that this situation occurs with frequency. It does not. However, a prisoner who can demonstrate that his advocate's presentation on his behalf was inadequate or ineffective will be given the benefit of a new trial. Therefore, the "right to counsel" for all definitely extends, practically speaking, to the right to effective, competent counsel for all. The right to a new trial is over and above the remedies that we discussed in the last chapter concerning possible steps to take against any ineffective attorney whether acting as advocate or counselor. Here we are talking about advocates in criminal cases, alone.

One problem that frequently occurs is that lawyers who defend clients who are convicted can be subjected to harassment by the ex-client. Any competent lawyer is perfectly willing to have his work examined by others to determine if he has performed in a creditable manner. This is not the problem. Although it is understandable, it remains a fact that prisoners often become convinced that their attorney handled their case incompetently. Jailhouse lawyers specialize in advising other prisoners how their case should have been handled. This often leads to a never-ending stream of legal challenges by the prisoners. An attorney who has done a perfectly acceptable job (many times without charging a fee) can be subjected to undue embarrassment by needless public questioning concerning his competence. The right to effective counsel should be structured so as to protect those attorneys who actually do give effective counsel.

Role of prosecutors and judges

As is true in many other legal situations, the role of the prosecuting attorney often can become obscured and misunderstood. He is not an avenging angel endowed with a call from on high to right all earthly wrongs and see that those who are guilty receive their just punishment. Though there are some grains of truth in this description, it is overly simplistic and for that reason, inaccurate.

The function of the prosecution is to see, in the name of the people, that justice is done. What is often lost sight of is the fact that there are many occasions in which justice can be accomplished only when the defendant is acquitted. If the defendant did not commit the crime with which he was charged, it would be an injustice of the highest order to find him guilty of so doing. The rights of the public at large are being served in the proper manner if the prosecuting attorney presents all the evidence legitimately at his command to the best of his ability. Then, it is up to the trier of fact, judge or jury, to decide whether the defendant in question has violated the rights of society in general, in the manner in which he is charged with so doing. Following this theory prevents the possibility of witch hunts. Most prosecuting attorneys are very careful in this regard. They have a fear of sending an innocent man to jail and consequently realize that their responsibility to the public stops short of the "guilty or else" stage.

An area in which prosecuting attorneys have great problems is withholding of evidence from the defendant that might enable him to prove his innocence if he knew about it. The reason that prosecuting attorneys are obliged to do this should be clear from the description of the role of any attorney as an "officer of the court." Justice will not be served if an innocent man is found guilty. Since the prosecuting attorney's primary function is to see that justice is done for the public, he cannot hide this evidence. Often the question whether the piece of evidence is unknown to the defendant and totally favorable to his side is hard to judge. It is rarely a black-

and-white situation and can be a difficult question of degrees. In this situation the prosecuting attorney could be violating his duty to the people to see that justice is done if he made the evidence known to the defendant. Since the prosecuting attorney is not the judge or jury, this places him in a hard spot. If he alerts the defendant to evidence that should be used to convict the defendant, he is violating his duty to obtain justice; if, on the other hand, he fails to warn the defendant and should, he is also preventing justice from being accomplished. This is a close question and much depends on the competence and sense of fair play of the district attorney.

The Old Testament in the story of Solomon talks convincingly about the difficulties of being a judge. These difficulties are too clear to need a great deal of explanation. Whether acting as interpreters of the law or as triers of the facts or both, it is necessary that judges more than anyone else see that justice is done. This is a great burden on any human being, since this judge is subject to irritability, prejudices, fatigue, poor memory, and many other imperfections like everyone else. Still it is necessary for the judge to rise above it and guarantee that justice is done. Only in this way are the rights of the people truly safeguarded.

As the decade of the seventies continues, it is becoming clearer and clearer that a small but loud portion of the population will not accept the verdicts of our courts as manifesting justice. It is questionable whether the fault lies with our court system. In fact, it seems far more likely that the defects may just as easily rest in the warped views of many revolutionaries. It must be remembered that a true revolutionary who objects to specifics in a system is not doing so to improve the present system, but rather because he desires to destroy it and establish some alternative.

In the face of hostility to the system on the part of defendants, the answer is not to deny them access to its protections merely because they disapprove of our courts. Some senators have suggested that those who show contempt for the legal system by disrupting it, forfeit their right to employ it. This is nonsense. Go back to our original guarantee of equal rights under the law for all. How could this exclusion be justified? We protect infants and insane people and see that they get equal rights even though they themselves do not know what they are. In a similar fashion, we must protect those who do know but do not accept. If we do not give equal treatment to those who do not want it, we will soon pass to the stage in which we will make arbitrary decisions as to those who do not want to make use of American justice and, therefore, should be denied access to it. At that point, oppression is just around the corner. Never before has our legal system been confronted in any noticeable number with defendants who do not wish to employ it to attempt to prove their innocence. This does not mean that the system is wrong and should be scrapped. In fact, it is a marvelous opportunity to demonstrate to all fair-minded people that this is a system with great merit that should be protected, defended, and strengthened.

The area of disruption of trials by the defendant was considered by the United States Supreme Court in March of 1970 in the Allen case; Justice Black, writing for the majority, handed down a very strict set of standards for dealing with this sort of problem. He said it was constitutionally permissible to bind and gag a defendant or punish him by holding him in contempt or by removing him from the courtroom until he promises to behave.

In addition to the judge's responsibility to apply the law, maintain order, and often to decide the factual questions as well, he is responsible in criminal cases for setting bail conditions and imposing sentence when necessary. These are all important duties.

Bail, which means that a defendant accused of a crime is allowed to remain free rather than rest in jail until his case is decided, is very important because of its humanitarian aspects. Also, it is proof of the often quoted boast that every American is innocent until proven guilty. Bail is in one sense a privilege, and in another sense a right. Again, we have to balance the individual citizen's right to freedom with the right of society to protection against wrongdoing. However, it must be kept foremost in mind that until pronounced guilty by a judge or jury at the end of a trial for an alleged violation of the criminal law, the accused is as innocent as you or I. It is for this reason, that whenever possible, the accused is released "on his own recognizance." This means he does not have to post bail. The court will accept his word that he will appear on the day his trial is scheduled.

Frankie Carbo, a well-known Mafioso boss of the forties and fifties, was the subject of the most important Supreme Court ruling on bail. Carbo, with the help of Chicago millionaire, Jim Norris, had muscled in on the boxing business. Through the International Boxing Club, Carbo and Norris tied up virtually all the fighers, managers, promoters, and radio-television rights to fights throughout the United States and Canada. If you did not play ball with Norris and Carbo, you did not play, period! Jack Leonard, a West Coast promoter who tried to buck the I.B.C., found out the hard way. The mobsters went so far as the dump lye in Leonard's swimming pool and call Leonard's wife on the phone to inquire as to the kind of flowers to send to her husband's funeral. When Carbo was indicted on criminal charges for allegedly violating the Hobbs Anti-Racketeering Act, the mob blamed Leonard and increased their terror tactics against him and his family. Carbo made an all-out attempt to get out on bail. To protect Leonard, the government objected to permitting bail in this case. This decision to deny Carbo bail, eventually reached the United States Supreme Court. Ruling on the bail petition, Justice Douglas upheld the denial of bail and set down guidelines to be employed in setting bail.

The key questions that a judge must determine are: (1) whether there is a likelihood that the defendant will escape before coming to trial; and (2) whether the defendant is liable to commit another crime while free on bail before a decision is reached in his trial. In the *Carbo* case, bail was denied for the second reason.

In order to answer these bail questions, it is necessary for a judge to refer to the past record of the defendant in order to make a correct decision. This should not be confused with using the past criminal record of the defendant at the trial to indicate guilt or innocence as to the crime in question. Bail is an entirely separate matter that has no bearing on guilt or innocence as to this particular crime. The only purpose for which the crime in question is relevant as to bail concerns the amount of money to be charged as security. If the defendant appears at the trial, the amount of bail is returned. Since the defendant has more to lose if found guilty of a serious crime, the bail is higher because the likelihood of escape is higher. As with almost all steps in the legal process, the amount of bail demanded or alternately the refusal to grant bail is reviewable by an appellate court which will look for a mistake in law or an abuse of discretion on the part of the judge ruling upon the bail application. The appellate court's reversal of Judge Hoffman's denial of bail in the "Chicago 7" case after their conviction, but during the time before their appeals would be decided, is an example of just such an overturning of a ruling in this area. Today higher courts more and more are demanding that the judge's ruling on bail be other than the trial judge. Obviously this would end later objections of a grudge by the judge against the defendants because the judge deciding the case knew the past record from the bail application.

The Vera Foundation has done wonderful work in New York to try to set up a workable system of bail for poor people who do not have enough money to post the bail bond. This is very important especially when courts are so crowded. Sometimes it is necessary to wait two years until trial in New York. Thanks to Vera, most first offenders without sufficent funds to post bail can continue their daily life and don't have to spend the long period before trial in jail. The trend for judges to set lower figures for bail in the case of first offenders is continuing. Many times, the judge will permit the defendant to remain free before trial simply on his promise to appear in court at the proper date. This is called technically: "a personal recognizance release." All this means is that the accused is personally responsible to see that he comes to court when his case is due to be heard.

Not all defendants live up to this promise to come to court

when their case is due. By the end of 1970, 177,000 criminal defendants in New York City were being sought for breaking bail. This is one-third of all the criminal defendants awaiting trial in New York City at that time. This is a very serious development. Courts will be less likely to let other defendants out on bail. The defendant will have a trial constantly hanging over his head and when he is found and tried, there will be a record of noncooperation that will count against him on the question of sentencing should he be found guilty. Jumping bail is a dangerous gamble.

The last major function of the judge, and in many ways his most difficult, is to pass sentence on a convicted defendant. In a very real manner, another man's whole life is in his hands. The judge is charged with vindicating the rights of an offended society, while at the same time imposing only that punishment which fits the crime committed. This is an extremely hard task especially with prisons in the condition in which they are. Jurists know that the percentage of lasting rehabilitation is small. In addition, the attitude of the general public toward an ex-con on his return to society retains strong resemblances to medieval attitudes of suspicion and shame. To knowingly send another human being to a jailbird's fate is a hard task. However, the safety of society demands that it be done. As best as he can, the judge is charged with fulfilling this obligation.

There has been some sentiment in recent years aimed at removing the burden of sentencing from the shoulders of the judge. The alternative seems to be the imposition of an indeterminate sentence with the duration left up to a board of review, rather than to the judge. There is some feeling that this procedure would emphasize the rehabilitative aspects of the sentencing process. Presumably this new board would act like and possibly even replace present-day parole boards. The goal would be to retain the prisoner in custody only so long as necessary to make him a productive member of society. This approach is not without its good points. In the overall picture, it still does not seem to be the answer. The norms for decision to be employed are too vague. What constitutes rehabilitation?

Who is to decide whether a person is sufficiently rehabilitated? What method is to be used? How much rehabilitation is enough? All of these pressing problems need a great deal more study before any adequate solution will occur.

At least for the short run, the present system of having judges pass sentences appears to be better adapted to the situation. Judges are vitally interested in rehabilitation and try to keep this aspect in mind when they sentence a prisoner. At the same time, the concept that society has been wronged and must be protected against further serious crime by the same individual is also very important. Sentencing is never going to be perfect no matter who does it. However, good judges —which by definition means that they are at the same time efficient, compassionate, informed, and competent—do a remarkably capable job in protecting the legitimate interests of society without at the same time extracting unjust retribution against the criminal.

Judges are totally aware of the problems encountered by convicts both during their imprisonment and after their release. For this reason, judges are very careful to weigh all the factors we have discussed above before sentencing a man to imprisonment. Even if the judge determines ultimately that the imposition of a jail sentence is absolutely necessary, multiple options as to length are still open. The judge is aware of the parole requirements in his jurisdiction. He knows down to the day how long a prisoner is liable to spend in jail before he is paroled for good behavior.

Sometimes parole and probation are confused in the mind of the public. *Parole* refers to a prisoner who is released from confinement before the full term of his sentence has ended. If the convict on parole fails to stay out of trouble, he can be returned to prison for the purpose of serving the rest of his sentence. *Probation* is similar to parole except for the fact that the prisoner on good behavior does not have to serve any part of his sentence. This also is known as a suspended sentence. As long as the convicted man fulfills the terms and conditions of his probation, his sentence will end without the necessity of actual confinement. Of course, this is a pleasant alternative. However, there have been abuses of discretion in permitting probation, especially with the young. In some states, as high a percentage of first offenders as 70 percent commit another crime later on. Presumably, most of these criminals received "suspended sentences" for their first offense. It is highly questionable if repeated suspended sentences in any way help either the convict or society. In most cases, when the man commits a second crime after mercy by the court, it is a poor sign for the future. Pessimistically, we might wonder if the frequent practice of granting probation for the first offense has helped the situation to any real degree.

One other area of sentencing that people often confuse concerns the distinction between *consecutive* and *concurrent* *sentencing*. This is another manner in which judges can regulate the actual amount of time that a man convicted of two or more crimes actually will spend in prison. If the judge passes sentence on each guilty verdict and specifies that the terms should run "concurrently," the speedometer starts on all offenses at the same time and runs out when the longest sentence has been served. However, if the sentences are to run "consecutively," they are served in order, one after another, from longest to shortest. To illustrate the difference, if a man is found guilty of rape, kidnapping, and robbery and is sentenced to 15, 10, and 5 years with all terms to run "concurrently," his time in prison will be up at the end of the 15-year sentence. On the other hand, if the judge orders that these sentences be served "consecutively," once the felon has finished the 15-year sentence, he must start to serve the 10-year sentence and after that the 5-year sentence. A judge has great power in the area of sentencing as the above situation demonstrates.

Our jury system

Unless the judge has decided the case himself and found the accused to be guilty, the only way that a case will reach the sentencing state is by a guilty verdict being delivered by a jury. Our trust in the decision of average citizens in criminal cases is one of the strongest points of American law. It is a

carry-over from the British system of government. This procedure is a real proof that we are a government of the people.
This is especially so in the area of jury decisions in criminal
law, since our entire basis for having criminal law statutes
is that the rights of the people have been violated by the
actions of an individual. Who better to decide if the rights
of all the people were violated, than a group of the people?

Juries are chosen from the list of voters for a town or city
in the area where a given court is located. All voters are
eligible except that it clearly would be improper to have people
such as lawyers, policemen, or judges. Given these few exceptions, everyone is eligible. Later on at the time of the trial,
the court is free to excuse those who have valid excuses such
as being ill, vitally needed at their jobs, a housewife with
small children at home, a client of any of the attorneys, or
a spouse or friend of any of the defendants or witnesses. Other
than these, everyone has a civic duty to serve on juries when
called.

Once the judge has determined that a prospective juror
will not be faced with a conflict of interests in the case, the
next concern is the mental attitude of the prospective juror.
If the prospective juror has formed an opinion on the case
from what he has read in the newspaper or seen on a TV
newscast or from discussions with friends or relatives, the
judge will excuse him if he reports that he does not have
an open mind on the subject and that his opinion is not subject
to change. If true, this honest admission by a prospective juror
is a great protection for a defendant charged with a crime
in a case that has received a great deal of pretrial publicity.
However, it must be recognized that many prospective jurors
have failed to fulfill their obligation as citizens by claiming
that they have a closed mind on the subject when in fact
they do not, but are using this as an excuse to avoid jury
service. It is better not to use these poor excuses for citizens
than subject the defendant to the possibility of a stacked deck.
The other mental attitude that would disqualify a prospective
juror consists in religious beliefs of a variety that would interfere
with the rendering of a verdict of guilty.

Even after a prospective juror has passed all tests of impartiality, he is still not out of the woods. All that has been so far established is that there is no preexisting reason preventing him from being a juror. Another way of saying this is that the juror cannot be "challenged for cause." Even though this is so, either the defense counsel or the prosecuting attorney can disqualify a certain number of jurors for any reason that comes to mind, such as: not liking their looks, their clothes, the color of ther skin, because a birdie provided a hot tip, or any other conceivable reason. These are called "peremptory challenges." They are totally up to the lawyers to use or not, and no reason has to be given by the advocate decided to use one. Naturally, the number of "peremptory challenges" are limited. Otherwise the advocate for the defense would keep disqualifying jurors all day long so as to prevent his client from being tried.

The jury system of this country is only as wise as the people of this country. The debates about the intelligence of jurors and the correctness of their decisions are endless and cannot be resolved. However, it remains a consoling thought that a man is convicted of a crime only when the twelve representatives of society as a whole say so.

A few states permit a guilty verdict if nine or ten of the twelve jurors vote for guilty. The Supreme Court has found this procedure constitutional. Because of the danger of error, it is hoped that no more states adopt a nine- or ten-juror guilty role. It is this extra step of condemnation by other ordinary citizens that makes our system of government different from others that emphasize police state tactics. A defendant in our society has a double option in determining the forum for society's judgment concerning his action. The defendant can choose to be judged either by a judge alone or by a jury. It is hard to conceive of a fairer method than our criminal law system for asking the forces of society to decide whether an act of the defendant is wrongful and deserves punishment.

The great emphasis placed on the necessity of condemnation by society in general as being the primary reason for treating an action as a crime has great bearing on a discussion of this topic. If the people do not feel that they have been offended, a crime has not been committed and the defendant should not be punished. If the reverse is true, the other side of the coin applies just as well. What actually offends society, changes. We saw the truth of this when talking about the differences between law and the legal environment. What the people of California considered to be kidnapping changed radically from 1901 to 1951. The same is true of marijuana. When the strict laws were passed prohibiting the sale, possession, or use of marijuana, society, acting through its duly elected legislators, thought marijuana was harmful to a very serious degree. This is why harsh penalties were placed in the laws. Today, the extreme harmfulness of marijuana is being questioned by many people in our society. If scientific studies demonstrate conclusively that the harm of marijuana has been overstated (this is by no means certain, especially in the area of psychological harm), it is likely that legislators will reduce the penalties in order to make them roughly equal to the actual amount of harm suffered by citizens. To fail to do so would violate the Eighth Amendment ban against "cruel and unusual punishment." It is a constitutional demand that the punishment must fit the crime.

What are criminal laws?

There is a difference between an offense against the public order (i.e., a crime) and an offense against the moral order (i.e., a sin). The state is out of its area of competence if it punishes a man for a sin rather than a crime. It is true that the same act may be at the same time criminal and sinful; however, the state must separate itself from the moral order except insofar as the offense against the moral order is also an offense against the public order. It is easier to discuss this subject in the abstract than it is to give concrete examples. The easiest example is abortion. However, it may not be correct. It may be that abortion violates the public order as much as it violates the moral order. The will of the people on this matter is not yet clear.

Crimes can be broken down loosely into crimes against a person and crimes against the property of a person. We are so familiar with them that there is no need to give examples. It might be helpful to clear up confusion concerning the justification for the same wrong being simultaneously both a criminal and civil wrong.

Civil wrongs are defined as violations of the rights of one person by *another person*. This is not the same as a *criminal wrong*, which is a violation of the rights of society by one person. How is it possible according to this definition that an assault and battery can be both a civil and criminal wrong? The answer is that the person assaulted it both an individual and a member of society. It is to society's advantage that each individual member be protected from assault. For this reason, criminal statutes are passed to protect the assaulted citizen. However, the penalty of imprisonment does not reimburse the victim for physical injury, loss of pay, hospital bills, frights, etc.; this is why a civil suit for money damages will provide an adequate remedy.

Although the same act against an individual can violate the rights of both an individual and society, it is necessary to keep them apart principally because the punishment differs. Since a violation of a criminal statute has as a penalty jail, the burden or proof demanded for conviction is higher than in civil cases. The state must prove its case "beyond a reasonable doubt" because of the presumption of innocence that attached automatically to all defendants in any criminal case. As we have said before, every man is innocent until proven guilty. On the other hand, for a civil wrong the punishment sought is money. It would be impossible to know on which party to impose the stronger burden of proof. For this reason, it is necessary to allow the parties to fight it out evenly. Therefore, the plaintiff in a civil case must prove his side by "a mere preponderance of the evidence." To illustrate concretely in our assault and battery example, assume that Joe belts Bill and breaks his jaw. Since Joe can go to jail for the criminal wrong committed, it is only fair that the state prove its case to a point where no reasonable doubt of Joe's guilt remains. In the civil suit by Bill against Joe, only money is at stake and both men come before the court with an even chance.

For this reason, a mere preponderance of the evidence will suffice. Bill has to prove his case only by showing slightly more evidence that he was wronged by Joe than Joe has to show that he did not wrong Bill. To say the same thing in another way: When the juror adds up the plus and minus columns in his own mind in trying to decide on a verdict, in a criminal case he has to be about 90 percent sure of guilt, but only 51 percent sure of his decision in a civil case, no matter which way he decides.

Summing up

Criminal law is a vast field full of good law, bad law, outdated law, obscure law, helpful law, and any other adjective you wish to supply. It would be a waste of time to preach to our readers about the advantages of observing the law. You would not be reading this book, if you did not want the law to help you. The temptations to commit crime are enormous in the ghetto. However, one small saving grace rises to the top. If a man gets in trouble, society will do everything possible to see that the rights of the defendant are protected and that he receives a truly fair trial to see if he committed the crime with which he is charged.

One might wonder by now as to the great emphasis on crime in this book. Well, it is true and we are going to spend another chapter and a half on it. The reason should be clear. A man who commits crime has no desire to make Urban Law work for him. The average citizen must be protected from him.

On the other hand, there is no area of the law where the poor have received more unfair treatment than in regard to our criminal laws. Today in a variety of ways we are trying to end this situation. Once the most evident type of legal discrimination against the poor is wiped out, we can work on other areas. We will then be sure that the government really wishes to help the poor and will give the poor the same protection and assistance to end the other areas of discrimination as it did in the area of criminal law.

Chapter 6

Ground Rules for Criminal Cases

Setting the scene

By this point, we all should have a fairly good idea of the role of lawyers and the type of protection that the United States citizen is guaranteed by our Constitution. We will look at the area which separates the men from the boys in deciding if the people of a particular nation are really free and their rights as citizens truly respected or not. Of course we are talking about the situation in which the police have strong suspicions that the citizen is guilty of a crime. What protection does the average citizen have and what chance to prove his innocence? We will see the answer in this chapter.

During the period that Earl Warren was the Chief Justice of the United States, great strides were made in making a reality for all criminal defendants of the rights guaranteed to all citizens by the United States Constitution. In its zeal to protect the public and punish wrongdoers, evils had crept into the whole area of the government's dealing with those accused of crimes. The Warren Court sought to insure equality in this area as well. This attempt was another proof of the basic principle that all Americans, even those accused of crime, have equal rights under the law.

Many citizens, especially those in the law enforcement area, were very critical of the limitations imposed by the Warren Court in criminal cases. With some justification they claimed that the restrictions made it far harder to convict criminals with the unenviable result that more criminals will be loose on the streets free to commit even more crime. There is some truth to this objection. Still, in the main, the police can live with these restrictions and perform their work with efficiency. In fact, the imposition of uniform standards can be helpful to them if they use them properly. Faithful application of these standards will decrease markedly the number of procedural mistakes that can result in reversals of convictions. More importantly than this, observance of the spirit of constitutional guarantees brings far closer to being a reality the concept that all are equal under the law. Once you draw a separate category as not being equal under the law (e.g., accused felons), it is very easy to extend this discriminatory category placing more Americans within it and denying to them their most basic rights as American citizens.

Search and seizure

Unless the police actually witness the occurrence of a crime, tips of other citizens are often the first lead which police receive as to the identity of suspects for the crime in question. When this occurs, the next logical step is to attempt to obtain evidence that will indeed prove that the suspects took part in the crime. This often leads to the search and seizure of evidence tending to show the accused actually took part in the crime. No one would deny that as the protector of the people, the police have a right and duty to search for matter that would link suspects to a committed crime. Only in this manner will society be protected from crime and the safety of its citizens preserved.

The duty of the police to find evidence for use in the prosecution of the accused must be balanced by the constitutional guarantee made to all citizens that they will be "free from unreasonable searches and seizures.'' The Warren Court sought to specify at what point a search became unreasonable. The reason for this is clear. Without restrictions in this area, visions of Nazi storm troopers breaking down doors in the middle of the night come to mind. Granted this is an exaggeration, but displays of poor judgment by the police have been known to occur, especially in ghetto areas. Criminal suspects still are citizens and have the right to be treated as such whether guilty or innocent. It is for a judge and jury to decide that they are guilty. This is not the business of the police. It is their duty to obtain evidence in a reasonable manner and arrest those who have possibly committed a crime.

Searches to obtain evidence for use in a prosecution fall into two distinct categories. These categories consist of searches that occur as part of an arrest and searches that occur before the suspect has been arrested. The crucial distinction is that a search made while a man is being arrested does not require the issuance of a search warrant by a court, whereas a search occurring at any other time does require a search warrant. By a *search warrant*, we refer to a legal step in which the state or federal law enforcement authorities obtain permission from a judge or his delegate to conduct a search of a specific area in order to attempt to locate and seize either the fruits of an illegal scheme or evidence that an illegal act has occurred.

There are two reasons for permitting a policeman to search the person and immediate area around a person arrested. The most important reason for permitting a search is to protect the policeman. In this day and age when so many of these brave men have been killed by criminals, no responsible person can object seriously to laws that allow policemen to search the arrested man and the area around him for weapons that might be used against the police in attempting an escape. The second reason for allowing the police to search without a warrant at the time of an arrest is to prevent the disposal of evidence that could be used against the accused. The fear is that friends of the accused could dispose of evidence tending to show the accused committed the crime in question before the police could return to the area of the arrest with a search warrant.

In this, as in all constitutional areas, the question soon appears as to how much is too much? Or in constitutionally correct search and seizure language: At what point do searches incident to an arrest become unreasonable? In the old days, any arrest was a come-on that permitted the police to range far and wide, inspecting almost everything within the county limits in the hope of finding incriminating evidence to link the accused with the crime which he was suspected of committing; or if not of that crime, then of some other hopefully more serious crime. Fishing expeditions were encouraged and though they sometimes succeeded, many times they did not. In any event, they were an unwarranted invasion of a citizen's privacy.

If a widespread search is needed, the proper procedure is for the police to return to court and seek a search warrant with as broad a search range as possible. Naturally, the police will need strong reasons to obtain this much authority from a court. The United States Supreme Court has tried to limit the acceptable area for a search occurring with an arrest to the body of the accused and the surrounding area near him. How far does this surrounding area concept extend? It would be foolhardy for us to try to decide. Each case must be judged on its own merits. In addition, the Supreme Court, as it should, keeps refining the concept of reasonableness to reflect the changing legal environment in which we in this country live. At the present time, a reasonable area for a search without a warrant appears to be the person of the arrested man and the room in which he is in at the time of the arrest. When we get a search that extends beyond this, the Supreme Court frowns. However, so far the Supreme Court still permits the search of the car and the car trunk if the man is arrested in or near his car. The fear is that a car itself or goods in it can be disposed of easily and that a search of the car in these circumstances is reasonable.

The other area in which a warrantless search occurring at

the time of an arrest carries the possibility of abuse concerns the validity of the arrest itself. Unless this area was restricted, it would be a great temptation for the police to trump up circumstances for an arrest so as to conduct a search without the necessity of proving the need for a search to the judge or the clerk of the court. Vagrancy, disturbing the peace, being a disorderly person, and loitering are some of the common catch-alls that come to mind readily. This is not to say that these are not legitimate violations against public order and safety. If they truly occur, it is legitimate to arrest and prosecute the offender. However, these charges are vague enough that abuses can occur. It is not proper to permit a policeman to search any person or place he wishes in the hope of finding some evidence of a crime. If unjustified arrests are permitted, this abuse will occur. The close inspection of the courts as to true probable cause for an arrest is a protection against the abuse of a citizen's rights. Still, it must be remembered that probable cause and conviction are not synonymous. It is not necessary that the person arrested be guilty of that or any crime. This is for a judge or jury to decide. It is only necessary that the policeman have reasonable cause to make an arrest from all the facts available. It can even turn out that the accused is not guilty of the particular offense for which he is arrested, and still the search will be upheld if the actions committed by the defendant were such that a reasonable man would have thought that there were sufficient grounds for an arrest. To sum up, a great deal of latitude is permitted in arrests justifying searches, but there must be some reasonable grounds.

Searches are much more closely regulated when they are made either before or after an arrest as opposed to occurring at the time of an arrest. It is necessary to obtain a court's permission for a search occurring at a time other than at the time of the actual arrest. To receive this type of search permission, it is necessary to convince the court that there is a reasonable chance that a crime has been committed; that the property to be searched is liable to possess the material sought; a detailed account of what is sought; and the story as to how the police came into possession of the information that leads them to wish to search the property in question. Usually this means that the state must reveal the name of its informant. This can hinder the police, but it is a further protection to citizens against unreasonable searches. The Supreme Court has gone so far as to invalidate seizures that find the wrong thing in the right place. The famous constitutional law case of *Mapp* v. *Ohio* is an example of this. The pornographic material that the police did not expect to find in its search was excluded. As the years go by, other problems and interpretations will occur in the search and seizure area. In individual cases there will be criticism that the courts are hampering the police unduly. This could be true. How hard it must be to judge what is "unreasonable." Still, it does seem better in the long run to be too strict in this regard, rather than not strict enough. Since search warrants are an extraordinary invasion of a citizen's privacy, they should be permitted with great caution. Unreasonable searches and seizures of the property of citizens can easily lead to oppression and police state tactics.

The other pretrial area which can lead to abuse and controversy concerns custodial interrogation and confessions. We have in mind the questioning of suspects by the police. At some point, the constitutional right to legal counsel and the constitutional right every citizen has not to give evidence against himself come into play. Unhampered questioning of possible felons by the police can, under some circumstances, interfere with these constitutional guarantees.

Just as it did in the area of search and seizure, the Warren Court also took significant action in the area of police questioning. Although, for the most part, tales of the "third degree" are exaggerated, it must be admitted that occasions have occurred in which excess zeal to obtain a confession has led to abuses of discretion by the police and a consequent denial of the defendant's constitutional rights. In a long line of cases ending with *Escobedo* and *Miranda,* the United States Supreme Court issued strict regulations to protect suspects from harassment. These are known familiarly as the *Miranda*

warnings. Their exact nature varies from state to state. However, the degree of difference is small. In essence they fall
into the following five categories: (1) A defendant has the
right to remain silent; (2) anything the defendant says can
be used against him in court; (3) the defendant has the right
to talk to a lawyer before and during questioning; (4) the
state will provide and pay for a lawyer at any time that the
defendant wishes if the defendant cannot afford one himself;
and (5) the defendant has the right to halt questioning at any
time and refuse to talk again until he obtains a lawyer.

Miranda established that the defendant has the right to use
any or all of the above guarantees simply because he is an
American citizen. It hardly needs saying that any alien on
American shores charged with a crime would also receive
the same constitutional protections. When must a defendant
be warned that he possesses these constitutional rights? Clearly,
no later than when he is arrested. This is the holding of *Miranda*.
However, if this were the only limitation on the police, they
could question at will before placing the suspect under arrest.
Obviously, this was not intended by the Supreme Court. It
is in this situation that the *Escobedo* case becomes important
because it provides the guidelines necessary to solve this problem. *Escobedo* does so by adding another important phrase
to the legal vocabulary, "the accusatory stage." This means
that once the questions of the authorities have crossed over
from the general informative area into the specific accusatory
area, it is necessary to warn the defendant of his rights as
stated in the *Miranda* case. To say the same thing in another
way, at the time the police stop asking a person questions
only to provide themselves with information useful in solving
the case and switch their line of questioning to areas in which
they hope that the one being questioned will admit participation in the crime, the accusatory stage has been reached.
If the police did not have to inform a defendant of his rights
at this point, a situation could arise such as did in *Escobedo*.
In that case, the attorney for Escobedo was denied the chance
to talk to his client though the attorney waited in the police
station for hours in the hope of being permitted to talk to

him. During this period, Escobedo was being questioned very vigorously by the police. Before the attorney was allowed to speak to his client, the police obtained a confession from him. The United States Supreme Court threw out this confession.

The right guaranteed to all of equal protection under the law can have strange results in this area. During the 1968 Detroit riots, three policemen were charged with shooting three black boys at the Algiers Motel. One of the policemen confessed shortly thereafter and explained his part in the incident in a written statement which he signed from a stenographic record taken at police headquarters. In the confusion caused by the riot, no one on the Detroit Police Department remembered to warn this officer of his *Miranda* rights before the confession was received. Because of this mistake, the confession was excluded and could not be used against the accused in court. Since there was not sufficient evidence against this policeman otherwise, he was never tried for murder. The court, and rightly so, held that the time at which the accused gave a confession to police whether spurred on by explicit questions or not, clearly was a time in which the case had reached the accusatory stage at which the policeman, now the accused, had to be warned of his *Miranda* rights like anyone else.

It might seem strange that a policeman who is expected to inform others of their rights would need to have them explained to him. A minute's reflection will show that under ''equal protection'' a policeman accused of a crime is no different from any other citizen. He can be just as scared, nervous, and upset as anyone else. Since this is so, it is just as important to remind an accused policeman of his most basic rights as a citizen as it would be to warn anyone else. Also, it sometimes is questionable if policemen really understand the nature of the *Miranda* warnings which some of them so glibly spout from memory. Again as in so many other areas, if you deny *Miranda* ''equal protection'' rights to some citizens (e.g., policemen), where do you draw the line? Lawyers should know *Miranda* rights. For that matter law students, newspaper crime reporters, even habitual criminals should know them. How can you fairly separate those who should be warned of their rights and those who should not? Also, how much chance is there that mental strain would cause an accused who should be expected to know his *Miranda* rights to forget them? Clearly, it is better to warn everyone at the time a case reaches the accusatory stage.

Suppose a case has not yet reached the accusatory stage, what protection does a person being questioned by the police have at this point? The answer, to be honest, is not much. It must be remembered that the police are charged with finding and arresting those individuals who have committed crimes against society. Although this duty is not as important as the constitutional safeguards guaranteed to every individual, we must realize that there are times at which the police must be virtually free so they can do their job as they see fit. A man who makes damaging admissions prior to the accusatory stage is held responsible for them. The most typical instance would be a person at the scene of a murder confessing to the police on their arrival. If the police have just arrived and still do not know what is going on, it is impossible to hold that they have reached the accusatory stage against any individual who takes it upon himself to confess. A similar occurrence happened in the Algiers Motel case. One of the other policemen involved made admissions concerning his part in the shootings during his duty report of the incident to superiors. The police report was written before the case against him had reached the accusatory stage. For this reason, admissions in the official report were admissible against him at his trial. Since no one has to testify against himself, a person does not have to make any statements to the police even in the nonaccusatory stage, regardless of whether his attorney is present or not. Of course, refusal to answer police questions is a foolproof way of transferring a case from the nonaccusatory stage to the accusatory one. An added problem occurs for anyone like a policeman who may be suspected of a crime and still must report the events that occurred as a part of his duty. Refusal to do so might cost him his job.

Just as clear as the right that an individual has not to make statements against himself is the right that a man has to make statements that will incriminate himself if he wishes. He can do this at any time, with or without his attorney's permission, just as he also can always consent to warrantless searches if he wishes. As long as consent is not obtained by the means of police promises that cannot be kept, the consent will stand. However, there is one exception to this rule that we will take up as part of the "spoiled fruit" doctrine.

The poetically named "spoiled fruit" doctrine is important both in the search and seizure area and in the pretrial interrogation area. Just as disease that has crept into one piece of fruit in an otherwise good container can infect the whole shipment of fruit, so also a search or pretrial interrogation that is constitutionally defective at the outset can infect and make worthless a perfectly valid search or pretrial interrogation that occurs later. The theory supporting this is that if the police had not gotten their foot in the door illegally, they never would have reached the stage where they would have enough information to carry out an otherwise perfectly valid search or obtain an otherwise unattainable admission. The Cleery case in Massachusetts illustrates this point. The Northhampton police searched a suspect's apartment for pornographic pictures without a warrant, without his consent, and not incident to an arrest. The police were successful in finding some obscene photographs and arrested the defendant later. After being booked at the police station, the defendant of his own free will brought the police back to his apartment and showed them another batch of pornographic pictures that they had not found in their first search. Because the original batch of pictures had been obtained by an illegal search, the Massachusetts Supreme Judicial Court excluded both groups of pictures on the "forbidden fruit" theory. The court reasoned that the defendant never would have consented to showing the police the second group of pictures if they had not found the first group. When the first group is eliminated as being seized illegally, it is not fair to use the second group against the accused either. This is a further indication of the importance of making the original search or interrogation conform to the safeguards set up to protect individuals. Not only can a mistake lead to the exclusion at the trial of the illegally obtained evidence or statement, but it also can infect otherwise perfectly good evidence that might be very valuable if the prosecution had started off on the right foot. The *Cleery* case is a perfect example of this.

Another area dealing with criminal law that has a great effect on urban dwellers and can lead to much worry on their part concerns arrest records and pretrial fingerprinting and picture taking and various other steps taken by the police to keep their records complete. Two areas of interest seem to conflict here as in so many other places in the book. On the one hand, involuntary fingerprinting, information gathering, photo taking, and the like are an infringement upon the rights of an individual citizen who at the time these procedures are carried out is not guilty of anything. However, society in general has a right to know who this man is. This will serve both to link him with other past unsolved crimes and also to provide a record of likely suspects for future crimes. It is on this theory that arrest records are retained, even if the defendant eventually is for some reason found not guilty. As long as abuses do not occur, this invasion of privacy seems justified.

A recent very important case, *Menard* v. *Mitchell*, decided by the Circuit Court of Appeals in Washington, D.C., seems to have struck the first blow to protect the good name of a ghetto resident who is arrested for a crime, but never convicted. The court was very concerned that the arrest record kept in F.B.I. files might be used against a man found innocent. Banks, insurance agencies, military authorities, and many other agencies can find out if a man was arrested and might deny him a loan, a job, a military promotion, or an insurance policy for that reason alone. Can we justify this with our belief that every man is innocent till proven guilty? It does not seem so.

Of course, there are many times when it is justified to keep prior arrest records as an aid to solving future crimes and also so as to know a true criminal's prior history. However, the court here questions whether it is fair to keep an arrest record if the police were clearly mistaken in arresting a man or if the police did seem to have reasons to arrest a man, but their later investigation showed they were incorrect. All urban dwellers should be happy that courts are finally dealing with the problem.

Physical exams of accused who are detained seem justified as a protection for the prisoner since he might be sick and need special care. Physical exams for a woman to determine whether she is pregnant have been justified on the special-care grounds as well.

Witness identification

The third area of pretrial activity that often causes confusion deals with identification of suspects by eyewitnesses. In many ways the problems in this area are the same as the problems dealing with search and seizure and pretrial questioning. In all three areas the very real fear exists that the desire of the police to build a case able to convict the defendant will interfere with the rights of the defendant that are his as a United States citizen. No area is more likely to lead to abuses than witness identification. We all are aware that mistakes can be made. Usually mistakes do not occur; however, they are possible. Neither the desire of the police to have the case closed nor the desire of witnesses to punish the defendant and reaffirm their own dignity should in any way hide the fact that it would be a miscarriage of justice if the identification was incorrectly made because of improper methods used by authorities.

In the last days of the Warren Court, positive steps were taken to insure that identification procedures employed by authorities satisfied basic criminal-law "due process" requirements. The primary manner in which this was accomplished was to permit the accused's attorney to be present at the lineup. This step goes a long way toward guaranteeing identification fairness.

There are any number of ways to influence the decision of a person who is attempting to identify a suspect. The shrewdness of some of these unfair methods is incredible. Other methods are very clumsy. Yet, they have one thing in common. All methods of persuasion try unfairly to stimulate the idea in the mind of the person making the identification that one particular person in the lineup should be identified.

If the witness to the crime testifies that he was assaulted by a black man, a lineup consisting of nine white men and one black man would be clearly unfair, even if this particular black man did not at all resemble the criminal who is sought. In the same manner, if the thug is identified as being tall, a lineup with nine five-footers and one man six feet, four inches tall would raise a legitimate suspicion that the police were rigging the identification so as to implant in the mind of the witness the belief that the one person in the lineup fitting the description that had been previously supplied is the man who beat him up. This power of suggestion should not be discounted. Psychologically, there is a pressure on the witness to identify someone. In an unspoken manner, an identification affirms the powers of observation possessed by the witness. To fail to recognize the accused in the lineup (if indeed he is in the lineup) carries a sense of failure that the witness unconsciously does not want to bear. Added to this is the natural desire of witnesses and more especially of victims to see that criminals are brought to justice. By bringing a criminal to justice, at least to this extent, the accused feels he has evened the score a little bit. All these considerations are powerful pressures that already cause any identification to be suspect. A "helping hand" by the police only increases the danger of error. The frequency of error in the area of identifications casts grave doubts that the requirements of criminal "due process" are being observed.

As in so many other areas, many close questions arise as to the fairness of lineup identifications. One sneaky example of police influence occurred in a case where an eyewitness was shown five different lineups. By the fifth lineup only the accused was still present from the original group. The appellate court sitting on this case reasoned that the witness may have been identifying the accused from his memory of him in previous lineups, as much as from his alleged memory of the assailant at the time of the crime. For this reason, the appeals court threw out the identification made by the witness at the fifth lineup. This holding seems justified because of the likelihood of mistake. If the eyewitness were so sure, why did it take five showings for him to pick out the man he selected as the guilty party?

Another case had permitted an identification to stand when a member of the lineup happened to wear the same color shirt as the robber had worn at the time of the crime. As we can see, the issue of basic fairness is a close one. How much difference is there between throwing out one identification because the accused was shown five times, and approving another identification in which the accused wore the same color shirt as the robber had at the scene of the crime? We are picking straws. The police are not charged with obtaining absolute equality in a lineup. To do so might defeat the very purpose for which the courts permit lineups. It would be possible to so equalize the members that no one could choose between them. Justice would not be served in this instance. However, as we have seen, the opposite extreme does not serve justice either. As in so many other areas, the rights of society to protection from criminals must be balanced against the right of the individual member of society to retain his innocence until proven guilty beyond a reasonable doubt. The high degree of possible error in lineups has led to a great reduction in their use by police in the last couple of years.

It would be wrong to leave the reader with the idea that identifications and lineups are exactly the same thing. They are not. At least for the present, one large identification area known rather loosely as "on-the-spot identification" means to bring a suspect before either the victim or an eyewitness shortly after the crime has been committed for a one-to-one meeting leading to the question: "Is he the one who did it?" The danger of mistake in this proceeding is easy to see. The emotional strain brought about by the crime is still very real for the eyewitness or victim, and this emotional strain may very well outweigh the advantages of having the identification made while the details of the features of the crook are still clear in the mind of the eyewitness or victim. The courts have permitted this sort of identification on the theory that it will be a protection to the accused permitting him to be shown to be not guilty at an early point in the investigation. (Optimists, are they not?) Of course, it is true that a quick decision will free a wrongly accused person from the fear of trial in the newspaper and community suspicion that he committed a crime. Nevertheless, it does seem questionable whether this benefit is enough to overcome the danger of the eyewitness or victim fingering the first person who comes in front of him.

It is true that society receives better protection by this one-to-one method. The police can center all their efforts on other suspects if the first one is not identified. Yet, it is questionable whether one-to-one identification should be permitted. Attorneys are not permitted at an "on-the-spot identification" on the theory that there is no time to obtain one, and that there is no necessity for his presence since the only question to be answered by the victim or eyewitness is: "Do we have the right man?"

Assuming that "on-the-spot identifications" are to be permitted in the future, two important questions arise. First of all, when is the time of the crime so far in the past that a one-to-one identification should not be permitted and either a lineup or some other form of identification must be substituted? Leading from this conclusion is the question as to the types of identification procedures other than a lineup that are permissible. Of course, as circumstances vary, the answers to these questions must adapt as well. Still, some guidelines can be suggested.

"On-the-spot identifications" are permitted if the case has not advanced to the point where a lineup would be practical. The theory for this is that the necessity of a lineup at this early stage in the investigation would cut down on the freedom and activity of the police. Clearly, when the case has reached the stage where someone has been formally charged with a crime, it is too late for a one-to-one "on-the-spot identification." However, such a meeting has been permitted when a policeman investigating an entirely separate auto accident in the evening called the owner of a liquor store who had been held up that afternoon, and had him come down to attempt to identify two witnesses to the accident whose descriptions were similar to that of the robbers in the previous incident. One has to wonder about the wisdom of this situation. Do we have to tell you that the accident witnesses were black?

Since an identification was permitted by the court on a one-to-one basis with a time lag from afternoon to evening, we should not be surprised that a recent case before the United States Supreme Court extended the time limit to two days. This *Kirby* case has been criticized and clouds this whole area. Other cases will be needed to end the confusion.

Even if the time necessary for the police to locate the suspect does extend the time limit allowable for a one-to-one identification to a point beyond a reasonable amount, there still are options open to the police. A lineup is not the only other type of permissible identification process. Mug shots can be shown instead, or a witness can be walked nonstop through a crowded police station, or a witness can sit in a chair while dressed as a policeman and observe all those who come into the station. In any of these instances, as long as the witness is not influenced unfairly by the words or actions of authorities, these identifications have been permitted.

Types of inadmissible evidence

Great stress in this chapter has been placed on the necessity of having searches, interrogations, and identifications follow constitutional standards. Any piece of evidence coming from a search, interrogation, or identification that fails to meet the due process requirements in these areas will not be permitted to be used in the court proceeding. There are many other types of evidence that for one reason or another fail to meet the standards necessary to be permitted to be used in the court case. Two of the most common types of evidence to fail this test are irrelevant statements and hearsay statements.

An *irrelevant statement* is one that does not have bearing on the point in issue and should not be allowed into evidence as worthy of use in determining the outcome of the case in question. To illustrate, the fact that Jones had a prior criminal record is not allowed to be used in a case in which the state is trying to prove that Jones had robbed the A&P. Jones' prior record proves nothing as to whether he did this particular caper. Therefore, it is not relevant to this particular case and would be highly prejudicial to Jones' chances of acquittal in this case. On the other hand, should Jones claim after he voluntarily took the stand in his own behalf that his previous record was good and offer this as an indication that he did not rob the A&P, his past criminal record would be extremely relevant and could be used by the prosecution to disprove Jones' claim that he was a lawful citizen. In fact, it would tend to prove the opposite.

Hearsay is the other important exclusionary device occurring in trials. It has as its purpose the elimination of any out-of-court statement offered into evidence by one other than the speaker in order to prove a fact or its contrary. For example, Tom testifies in court that Bill told him that he had seen Ed rob a bank. The reason for excluding this type of statement should be obvious. There is no way for Ed's advocate to cross-question Bill since he is not testifying. This brings up a double evil. Tom might have misunderstood the statement or made up all or part of it. The other possible difficulty is that Bill might have lied or been mistaken. However, since Bill is not on the witness stand, there is no way to find out. It would not be fair to permit a judge or jury to give evidence of this type much weight when deciding a case. There is a very real possibility that the statement could be incorrect and remain undetected. On the other hand, it would slow down the process of justice if out-of-court statements were excluded for all purposes. Exceptions are permitted, but it is beyond the scope of this book to spell out the various times when exceptions to the hearsay rule are permitted in court. It should be enough for our purposes merely to point out a couple of the most common: admissions and prior inconsistent statements.

Admissions are prior statements made by the defendant that tend to indicate his guilt. For example, Tom says in court that Ed told Bill yesterday that he had found $250,000. Anyone can testify to this fact. A *prior inconsistent statement* is a statement made by a witness or defendant in the past that conflicts with the present position taken by the witness or defendant while testifying in court at this time. Anyone can testify to the prior inconsistent statement. For example, if Bill told Tom the next day that Ed had a Luger in his hand, Tom could testify in court to this out-of-court statement to disprove the courtroom testimony of Bill that Ed had a Magnum pistol in his hand when he robbed the bank. Naturally evidence of this sort should be admitted even though it is an out-of-court statement, since it tends to disprove the present testimony of the witness and has a direct relationship to the guilt or innocence of the defendant. Keeping all statements of these types out of a courtroom are further protections to the defendant and assurances that he will receive a fair trial.

Summing up

The police don't seem to have come off too well in this chapter. This is a false impression. The very high percentage of all policemen are wonderful, brave, compassionate citizens who do an extremely difficult job in a fine manner. The best study done on police and the difficulties of their task is by John R. Lambert for the Oxford University Institute of Race Relations. It is called *Crime, Police and Race Relations* and is about police work in English slums, but almost everything in it applies to the American scene.

We underrate our police and their willingness to do justice. Groups of concerned citizens should meet with the police. Talk over the problems and try to work together better in the future. Sometimes it is surprising what a little consideration and willingness to take the first step will do. It can't hurt to try.

Chapter 7

Legal Status of Juveniles

Setting the scene

There are a number of men walking around the streets these days in $300 suits because they have convinced everyone they are experts on youth. Psychiatrists, school system superintendents, legal foundation directors, H.E.W. supervisors, etc., are all well paid to deal with youth problems. With so many experts, one wonders why it is necessary to devote a chapter in this book to juveniles. The answer is simple. The theorists have not come up with all the answers. It is not all their fault. If parents don't do their share, it is almost impossible for parental substitutes to fill the gap. The trouble which this country has with youth today will surely become problems with the adults of tomorrow. We aren't going to waste time by balancing the books with the tales of the numerous good youths in this country. We all know that. The point is there are many who aren't. These are a danger to the rest and steps must be taken to change this situation.

The most obvious solution is at the family level and the need for teaching good, wholesome values at an early age cannot be overemphasized. However, if failure occurs here, law must come into play to protect the rest of society. Still, at an early age, a juvenile can often be saved if the law treats him wisely and fairly. Nowhere is this more true than in the big-city areas. The first time the youth has trouble with the law is its big opportunity to show him by fair treatment that it would rather not be dealing with him and that if he goes home and behaves himself, the law will be happy. This wise approach wasn't always used in the past. However, it is clear today that the only way to possibly save the situation from a legal point of view is to say to the youth: "Listen, pal, we will treat you fair, so treat us fair!" If this happens, potential good citizens who can make Urban Law work will be saved and not left to rot in prison. This chapter will show how the law attempts to be fair to juveniles.

The first hint of trouble

In 1961 Washington, D.C., had a statute dealing with the ticklish question whether juveniles over sixteen and under twenty-one should be tried as juvenile delinquents or as adult offenders. This statute, said a Juvenile Court judge, must make a "full investigation" before deciding whether the youth should be tried as an adult offender or a juvenile offender. No guidelines were given as to the elements necessary for a "full investigation."

Morris A. Kent, Jr., was sixteen years old at the time of his arrest. The Juvenile Court judge decided he should be tried as an adult. Then Kent was indicted as an adult offender on three counts of housebreaking, three counts of robbery, and two counts of rape. Legal counsel for Kent had unsuccessfully attempted to obtain a hearing before the Juvenile Court judge decided whether Kent should be tried as an adult or a juvenile. This motion was denied. The attorney for Kent asked also to be allowed to read the previous juvenile court record and reports concerning Kent and to read the results of the mental exam made in connection with the present case. He was refused permission to do either.

Which court was to try Kent was a crucial question since Kent could receive a life sentence if he were tried, convicted, and given the maximum sentence as an adult. However, if tried as a juvenile, Kent was liable to commitment as a juvenile offender. Since this commitment must end by law when he reached twenty-one, Kent would be subjected as a juvenile deliquent to a maximum of five years' detention. For this reason, the stakes riding on the Juvenile Court judge's decision were high. The question of the fairness of the method used to decide the court question became important because Kent was found guilty of all housebreaking and robbery counts and was sentenced to prison terms that could extend from thirty to ninety years. Finally, the method employed to decide the court question in the *Kent* case reached the United States Supreme Court for its review. Justice Abe Fortas wrote the majority opinion in *Kent* and held that the method employed by the Juvenile Court judge to decide the court question was improper and made a reversal of the adult convictions of *Kent* necessary.

Nine-tenths of the importance of *Kent* lies below the surface. To save itself from becoming bogged down, the United States Supreme Court historically has worked on the theory that it will not decide the broad issues in a case if its decision can rest on more narrow grounds. This occurred in *Kent*. All that the Supreme Court decided was that Kent did not receive a fair hearing on the question as to whether he should be tried as an adult offender or a juvenile offender. It is shocking and hard to believe, but it is the truth that only one judge was assigned as a Juvenile Court judge in Washington, D.C., in 1961. Surely, the calendars of this court were overwhelmingly crowded with untried cases. No wonder the judge refused to give a hearing to the counsel for Kent. It is also highly doubtful that a man with this sort of workload could under any circumstances give "the full investigation" demanded by the statute whatever that meant, since the term was not defined. Even if the judge could make a full investigation himself, it is questionable whether basic due process grounds would be met if he denied the attorney for the juvenile access to the records and also refused to give him a chance to argue against a trial as an adult offender.

Gault to the rescue

Kent is just one small example of the mess that the country was in ten years ago concerning the rights of juveniles. *Kent* was a hint of things to come. It did not take long for the problems hinted at in *Kent* to rise to the surface. They did so in the next term of the Supreme Court in the case of *Gault* v. *Arizona*. There were no narrow grounds on which *Gault* could be decided while still preserving the concept of juvenile rights as they stood at that time. There was no easy way out in *Gault* as there had been in *Kent*. The weaknesses of the juvenile court system were exposed in all their ugliness for everyone to see.

Gerald Gault, a fifteen-year-old boy already on probation from an Arizona Juvenile Court for being present where a handbag had been stolen, was arrested along with a friend for making an obscene phone call to a woman living in the neighborhood. Justice Fortas termed it a call in which "the remarks or questions put to her were of the irritatingly offensive, adolescent, sex variety." In a Juvenile Court proceeding, Gerald was sent to a detention home for an indefinite period that could have lasted until he reached twenty-one, that is, for six years.

In many ways, *Gault* was the reverse of *Kent*. Gault was tried as a juvenile delinquent. Kent was tried as an adult. If sentenced as a juvenile, Gault could be held for up to six years. The highest possible adult sentence for Gault's offense was six months; Kent was sentenced for a term of up to ninety years as an adult, whereas five years was the maximum that he could be contained as a juvenile. However, one important factor in Kent and Gault is identical. They both showed the vast unfairness in the juvenile court system and a consistent pattern of denial of constitutional rights to juveniles. Justice Fortas traced the history of juvenile rights at the start of the *Gault* case.

In light of this history of juvenile courts, it is reasonable to question if Gault or Kent or any juvenile really receives his constitutional rights as a defendant. To say that a juvenile delinquent is not actually a defendant is ridiculous. Gault and Kent were imprisoned in institutions for offenses they were charged with having committed. If this is not a criminal proceeding, it certainly does share most of the earmarks of one. Anyone who needs further proof that the punishment is criminal should read in the papers about the Lollis incident in New York where a fourteen-year-old girl was placed in solitary confinement for two weeks dressed only in night clothes and without reading matter or possible recreation. What is even sadder was that she was in this detention center because of her parents' neglect, not for any crime she might have committed.

In juvenile matters, where do we go from *Gault?* Two different trends have shown themselves in the short time since *Gault* was handed down. As might be expected, there has been a steady succession of cases strengthening and explaining fully the rights of juvenile delinquents. The United States Supreme Court recently decided in the *Winship* case that juveniles are entitled to the same burden of proof in a criminal trial as would be an adult defendant. No longer can a juvenile be found guilty upon a mere preponderance of the evidence. Just as in an adult case, it will be necessary for the state to prove guilt beyond a reasonable doubt. We explained the meaning of these terms before. They should now be applied in the same way in criminal juvenile trials. This leaves only the right to a jury trial. It is doubtful that this right will be denied to a juvenile for much longer. Given the other decisions in this area and their rationale, it does not make sense to deny to the juvenile risking imprisonment the benefit of trial by jury. However, the first time that the United States Supreme Court faced this problem after *Gault*, the justices decided to leave to individual states the choice whether to provide for jury trials for juveniles. It is hoped that the next time they face this question, they will order all states to provide for jury trials for juveniles.

The second trend in juvenile affairs that follows hand in hand with the first may not be as desirable. The reasoning for it follows like this. If you extend all the constitutional privileges of being an adult to an infant, you should go all the way and treat him in court as if he were an adult. To do so, it would be necessary to abolish our juvenile court system as it presently stands. Therefore, the two trends taken together have as a goal to make a criminal juvenile just like an adult in all matters except punishment.

The first idea of giving all criminal rights to juveniles is easy to see. In pre-*Gault* days, the courts always kept the juvenile delinquent's name out of the papers while at the same time not giving him all his criminal rights. In actuality, the silence concerning the proceedings that occurred might be better abandoned if the disgraceful situation demonstrated by cases such as *Kent* and *Gault* could have been exposed earlier. *Gault* did not prevent special treatment for juveniles. It is still possible to keep the account out of the daily press. What *Gault* did prevent was treating a juvenile as a criminal defendant without giving him the rights of a criminal defendant. Thus since *Gault*, as long as you give the juvenile his basic rights, you can give him added protection as well if you desire. You can put as much whipped cream on the pie as you wish, so long as the pie is present on which to have it rest. In the past, the situation often was more like catching whipped cream smack in the face without any pie with it.

The extra protections for a juvenile can be as extensive and far-reaching as deemed necessary. Keeping this in mind and falling back on the old and partially true saying "that there is no such thing as a bad boy," it is possible to invent a system that would keep mentally disturbed juveniles and noncriminal problem children out of court at all. This would leave the courts for truly criminal delinquents. One of the great problems with our overcrowded and overworked juvenile court system is that too many children are brought into this court who have absolutely no business being there. If the screening of mentally disturbed children were better, discovery of mental illness would be easier. Although the cost and operational problems involved with mental examinations for all juveniles charged with crime would be very high, this procedure would have tremendous advantages. Too often mentally disturbed children go undetected when they commit minor criminal offenses. The unchecked mental illness later leads to more serious criminal acts. It would be worth the expense to the state to aid these mentally ill children at the outset and not treat them as if they were criminals. There are plenty of truly criminal juveniles without them.

The same reasoning that applies to early discovery of mental health problems applies equally to early discovery of behavioral difficulties and assigning children with them to family counselling and other community agencies of this type. Too often juvenile courts are improperly asked to deal with behavioral problems such as being a stubborn child or a truant. The court system does not belong in this area. The juvenile courts have neither the facilities, procedures, nor penalties available to deal with conduct of this type because it is not truly criminal in scope. The courts cannot play parent or social worker effectively.

The treatment received by Gault was a farce, yet unfortunately it is a farce repeated over and over in juvenile courts. At the time of the *Gault* case, 7,000 juvenile cases were on the call list awaiting a hearing in the city of Philadelphia alone. Court calendars of 70 to 80 juvenile cases a day before a single judge are common in large cities. Until 1970, the State of Massachusetts had only one separate, distinct juvenile court; and Washington, D.C., at the time of *Kent* also had one juvenile court. With overcrowding such as this, it is no wonder that cases such as *Gault* or *Kent* could have happened. It is a frightening but important question to inquire as to how many other Gault type cases have occurred that didn't have a happy ending. Before trying to suggest some solutions, it will be worth our time to examine closely the procedural constitutional guarantees denied to Gerald Gault.

The first constitutional right denied to Gault was the right to receive adequate notice of charges to be brought against him. The chain of events happened in the following order. On Monday, Gault was arrested. On Tuesday, Gault's parents were told of his whereabouts. On Thursday, the parents received a notice that Gault's case would be heard the following Monday; and that Gerald would be charged with the specific offense of being "a delinquent minor and that it is necessary that some order be made by the Honorable Court for said minor's welfare." It is impossible to prepare a defense in a few days, especially if you are not told exactly what is the offense that you are supposed to have committed.

The second constitutional guarantee denied to Gault was the right to legal counsel. The parents were never told that they had the right to employ a counsel or have one appointed by the Court and paid for by the state, if the parents were unable to afford one themselves. This is an extention of the "right to counsel" that was guaranteed to all criminal defendants by the *Gideon* case. In *Gault*, the Supreme Court comes very close to saying that a juvenile delinquent is a criminal defendant.

Third, since the woman who claimed that Gault had made an obscene phone call to her did not have to be present at the hearing, the constitutional right to face your accuser and to cross-examine him or her was not present. The Supreme Court objected to this as well. It is entirely possible that what one woman thinks was an obscene call might not seem like an obscene call to a judge that would call for a sentence of up to six years in a juvenile detention home.

The fourth objection was that a confession was taken from Gault without warning him of his *Miranda* rights to remain silent and to consult with an attorney before making any statement. The confession taken before he could consult with anyone was used against Gault at the juvenile hearing. The Supreme Court objected to this as well.

For all the above reasons, *Gault* was reversed. Thus, in one large leap juveniles have been hauled up by the bootstraps and guaranteed most of the rights that are preserved for an accused adult. When you consider that a juvenile detention home is in many ways just another jail, this seems only right. This is especially true when we consider that Gault could be sentenced to a detention home until he reached the age of twenty-one for the making of an obscene phone call. In Gault's case this could amount to a total sentence of six years. On the other hand, even without parole, an adult charged in Arizona with the same crime of making an obscene phone call could be sentenced to a maximum sentence of six months. Because of weird results such as this, it clearly is time to insure procedural due process for all juveniles.

At the present time it is safe to say that the whole idea of a separate juvenile court is under study. In the past we have dumped too much responsibility on the juvenile court. Actually, the main problem is not whether there will be a separate juvenile court or if its work load will be made part of the adult court system. No matter which occurs, the same rules must be used in the future. What remains as the most important objective in the area of juvenile treatment is to utilize effectively professional counselling and psychiatric assistance in order to catch criminal mental or behavioral problems at the start. If this is done, there is a far greater chance that juvenile crime can be controlled than presently exists. *Gault* will guarantee procedural due process to minors. It is a black mark on American justice that this state of affairs took so long to occur. Although the greatest focus in this chapter is on the criminal activities of juveniles, there are other areas in which juveniles traditionally have been treated in a different legal manner than adults. Education is one of the most important.

Legal rights of students

As far as schools are concerned, it is only within the last ten years that students have become real human beings. Before that time, students were in many ways a mere educational instrument to be instructed and manipulated like a mere piece of wood. This is no longer the case. The concept that a college acts in any sort of a parent-child relationship to its students has long since been blown out of the skies. Situations such as *Gott* v. *Berea College*, a 1913 Kentucky case which upheld the right of a college to forbid students from eating away from the campus at a neighboring restaurant, would not be tolerated today.

Today it is acknowledged that all schools are institutions and not parents. Schools have the same right as any other institution to pass and enforce rules to carry out its duties and to protect the safety of its employees and customers. However, this is a far cry from being a parent. It must be remembered that today the law recognizes that students are citizens. This implies that all the laws applying to other citizens apply to students and demands a fair application of all laws to them as well. However, a country that permits and thereby seems to encourage lawlessness for students is headed nonstop upon evil days. Student unrest is beyond the scope of this book and remains a very difficult subject. Still, dangerous storm clouds lurk for all, rich or poor, if the young generation as a whole decide that actual violence of any form is an acceptable way of bringing about change in this country.

High-school affairs retain a far closer resemblance to the old parent-child relationship than college situations do. Still, the inroads into this relationship are substantial in the high schools. From long haircuts to mini skirts to demonstrations for tenure for teachers, it is clear that the old state of affairs is a thing of the past, never to be revived. As with colleges, there is the same problem of the responsibility of the school toward participants in their programs. Any institution has the obligation to see that the atmosphere in the school makes it possible to supply the services promised. This applies as well to businesses, but has even more importance when dealing with schools. Without some degree of order, no school will function. Totally apart from the question of substitute parental care, there is the deeper obligation of the school to furnish the service promised; because in reliance upon this promise, the students, parents, or taxpayers of the state have paid their funds. Some regulations are necessary to balance the need for good order with the constitutional rights of the individual.

A New York court has allowed a college student to recover

part of his tuition when the private college he attended shut down for a few days to protest a political action of the government. This case was overruled by a higher court, but it still should serve as a warning to colleges. Also a judge in Ohio became so disgusted at the arguing between the parents of a long-haired fourteen-year-old and the school authorities, that he said everyone in the case was acting as if they were fourteen years old. These two cases can teach us a good lesson. Adults ought to act like adults. There are areas where one says "what I do is of fundamental importance no matter what"; and there are other areas in which stubbornness and selfishness must give way to the good of the greater number. Being a true adult demands acting like one when convenient and not convenient. It's ridiculous to demand that youth act like adults, when actual adults won't do so.

The student is not always in the wrong in his disputes with school or college administrations. It is an absolute necessity to receive proper education in order to obtain a good job. If a student is prevented from going to school, wrongly, the administrators in question are responsible for keeping that man underemployed or even unemployed for the rest of his life. The courts recognize that educational administrators need freedom in handling problems with students, but still will demand that an elementary sense of fairness and justice be observed by these administrators.

Especially in the case of younger students, many courts are stepping into the picture in situations in which they would have left the dispute in the hands of school administrators only a few years ago. One example is the case of pregnant high schoolers. A few years ago, this would have been grounds for immediate expulsion in most high schools. Today courts have insisted that these girls receive the same schooling as everyone else and the Massachusetts Supreme Court has gone so far as to insist that a pregnant girl be allowed to take all classes in the same classroom as the rest of the students, for as long as possible. In other instances some courts have demanded recently that parents be given notice and explanations for the suspension of their children and the chance to demand a hearing to present their side to the case and try to work out a compromise. A Washington, D.C., court has blocked the publication of the names and test scores of problem students. This information was contained in a Congressional subcommittee report. The court held this was a violation of the child's privacy. In like manner, courts have upheld the right of students to say what they wish in a school paper without prior censorship by the administration. To do otherwise would violate the students' rights to "freedom of speech" and "freedom of press." This of course does not mean that they couldn't get in trouble either criminally or civilly for what they wrote, after they distributed it; but only that they cannot be blocked from saying it if they desire to do so. In all the examples we have used, the law differs from court to court and state to state. However, one thing is very clear. The winds of change are blowing and they are favorable winds for all students, from rich and poor families alike.

Battered, neglected, and abused children

One of the saddest sights witnessed by doctors and nurses in hospitals is the cases of "battered children." This term describes those infants who are brought to a hospital after being beaten up, usually by one of their parents. It is very strange, but a certain class of unworthy parents enjoys taking out its frustrations by punching, kicking, burning, or beating with a stick or coat hanger one of their own children or the child of a lover. Until recently, both medical and law enforcement authorities have felt extremely helpless when they try to assist this type of child. Rarely do any witnesses appear. The child is too young to tell what happened. So whatever lie is cooked up by the parent, such as a fall or that the child burned himself, is very hard to disprove. Unless the incidents are repeated so often that added hospitalization is necessary, there has been little that could be done. There is not enough evidence for criminal prosecution of the parent or a "care and protection proceeding" to have the child removed from the parent on either a permanent or a temporary basis. In fact, until now the hospital did not have the authority to keep the child for medical attention if the parent demanded at any time that the hospital return the child to her. This often happened once the parent could see that the child would not die.

Recent legislation in many states has sought to improve the bleak picture regarding "child battering." Forward-looking legislation in some states permits hospitals to retain custody of a battered child if they wish for a reasonable length of time, usually ten days, no matter what the parent wants. The purpose is to have adequate time to help the child. Procedures for reporting cases of "child battering" to the police or child protection agencies are being improved and made mandatory on doctors and nurses. Some doctors have objected that this would be a violation of the doctor-patient privilege, but the better view is that everyone, even doctors, must report the seeming occurrence of a crime. It is not up to the doctor to determine guilt. Mandatory reporting will enable interested agencies to institute criminal proceedings or to watch the home situation closely in hopes of preventing a reoccurrence.

If the "battered child" will be protected by our society, what about a child who is brought into the world as illegitimate or deformed? Does such a child have a right to sue for damages he has suffered? As to illegitimates, the Illinois Supreme Court has said no, in the famous *Zepeda* case in which an illegitimate child through "his next best friend" (a legal term to describe the person who actually brings a suit for a minor) sued the putative father for damages suffered by being brought into the world as a result of a union outside of wedlock. The putative father in this case was married to another, so this child was the result of an adulterous relationship. The court agreed that a wrong had been done to the child, but said that if they permitted this sort of suit, they would be opening the door to an enormous number of suits by children who were brought into the world under objectionable conditions. Besides illegitimacy, the court had specifically in mind children brought into the world into total poverty. The theory here would be that such parents should not have children they cannot afford.

The court felt that if such wide-reaching types of personal injury suits were permitted, they should be specifically authorized by the legislature. This is a proper decision when we recall the discussion of the function of a legislature that was covered in the *Knowles* and *Chessman* cases.

Although legislatures have not provided for money damages for illegitimates, they have moved in other ways to lessen the plight of these unfortunates. States are very quick to declare officially that these children are legitimate if the other spouse accepts the child as being its own even though this objectively could not be the case; or if the party with the child marries, the child will be declared as a legitimate offspring of that relationship even if this objectively could not be true. Also, in areas such as inheritance an illegitimate child has received great assistance in recent years.

It is an unfortunate by-product of the overpublicized and overstated but nonetheless existent "sexual revolution" that far more illegitimate children are occurring then in the past. Possibly legislatures will feel that the damage to the child caused by being born out of wedlock is sufficient to provide a cause of action. One area in which suits may be permitted are birth defect cases. There is no sadder sight than to see a child who will go through life with some terrible handicap because of a birth defect. The parents usually are not at fault and deserve our fullest sympathy and assistance. Yet, suppose the parents are at fault. More and more evidence comes to the fore of the frighteningly high incidence of birth defects in children of women who have taken L.S.D. If a direct relationship can be proven, this might be a very good area for permitting a personal injury suit by the child born with a defect.

The whole area of adoptions and care and protection proceedings is being redefined today, both to extend true due process and equal protection to all concerned and to see that the best interests of the child are protected. These are agonizing decisions for a judge: in an adoption case, who should be made the legally responsible parent for the child, and in a care and protection matter whether the home atmosphere is so bad that the child should be removed and placed in another situation of the court's choosing. These areas are changing rapidly, and it would be dangerous to say more than the fact that the change and discussion taking place is all to the good. The fairer the system becomes, the more the child will benefit. Naturally, this means society will benefit as well.

In summation, it is becoming clear that the ideal of "the best interests of the child" is evolving rapidly in many areas. Our society is becoming more conscious of the true meaning of the phrase, "best interests of the child," and is trying to see that these interests will be protected in reality. With youth demanding so much in many different areas, it is absolutely necessary to treat them as much as possible like adults. As with any other human relationship, added privileges carry with them added responsibilities. Hopefully, this fact will be accepted by youth and they will act accordingly.

The added responsibility of youth will change many legal areas. In the past, courts have allowed a minor to refuse to pay any contract for nonnecessaries. The theory was that an unscrupulous merchant could trick a minor into buying merchandise he did not need. Especially in long-term contracts, the minor could fall into serious debt. For this reason, any contract of a minor for other than a necessity of life could be written off at the discretion of the minor. To further punish the unscrupulous merchant, the minor was able to retain the merchandise or services agreed to in the contract. It is highly questionable today as to who is the sucker. Too many youngsters with questionable morals are taking well-meaning honest merchants to the cleaners by stating or pretending that they are twenty-one and then cancelling the contract while still retaining the goods. It has become so bad that many courts are stretching the definition of a "necessity" way beyond acceptable bounds in order to protect the merchant. It would seem to be better to drop the concept and treat fraud in this area like fraud in any other. In other words, if you want to act like an adult, you will be treated like one.

Two other areas in which privileges and responsibilities for juveniles should be balanced are the eighteen-year-old vote in all elections, not just federal as the law now stands, and the eighteen-year-old drinking age. Given today's conditions, these actions would both tend to have far more positive effects than negative. A large sense of frustration on the part of those in their late teens would be eliminated. Hopefully, the concept of equal privileges and equal responsibilities will touch all areas of dealing with juveniles during the seventies.

Summing up

No generation has been talked about, analyzed, scolded, or praised as much as the present group of youngsters. One thing is sure. It is their country tomorrow. They are the ones who will make the laws, elect the government, and observe the laws. They are our insurance policy and our future. We must do everything possible to make this a good country for them. A country they will desire to love, protect, and perfect. For this to happen we must treat them fairly, educate them well, and give them goals of which to be proud. This, of course, is easier to say than to do. However, fair treatment in courts and schools is a start. If we play fair with our future citizens, chances are very good that they will do the same with us.

One final word to end this chapter, and this is a very ugly word: "drugs." The reader might wonder why we haven't covered this problem when talking about either criminal law or juvenile law. The point is well taken, but the answer is that criminal and juvenile laws are only the final resting place of our drug problem. Other government agencies must stop the problem before it reaches the poor victim who commits crime to support his habit. In Chapter 11, we will examine these drug-prevention steps in detail.

Chapter 8

Urban Housing

Setting the scene

Until urban poor obtain adequate housing, our nation's goal of true equality for all citizens will never be a reality. It would be silly to take the time to prove that those living in slum housing are disadvantaged. If a man must live in a dump resembling the cage of an animal, why is it surprising that he acts like an animal? Of course, this can be an oversimplification and has been hidden behind to attempt to excuse many examples of lawlessness. There is a vast difference between poverty living in New York's Harlem or Philadelphia's south section on the one hand, and the relatively less crowded Roxbury area of Boston or the Watts area of Los Angeles. True, poverty occurs in all these areas; but conditions are far more cramped and restricted in some than in others. Blanket sympathy for criminal actions supposedly motivated by crowded housing conditions is suspect. Society exists in the ghetto just as in the rich suburbs, and those living in the ghetto have an equal interest in seeing that their rights are protected. Otherwise, all cities will be total jungles.

What to do about housing? Even Thomas Jefferson might be stumped at this problem. Some people own houses and

119

others do not. Virtually all landlords other than the government are in the housing business to make a profit. This only stands to reason. Before we get into any detailed examination of housing or landlord-tenant affairs, it is absolutely necessary to keep the basic truth of the situation clearly in mind. The more the landlord can take in as rent while at the same time spending the least amount of money possible in upkeep, the more his profit. This almost inevitably makes landlords and tenants enemies.

The natural tension existing between a landlord and tenant is' even greater in big-city areas. This is doubly true when the landlord is an absentee landlord, especially if of a different color. Given the fact that a landlord primarily wants money and a tenant primarily wants a nice residence, it follows inevitably that the poor who do not have money enough to go elsewhere are forced to accept what the landlord gives them. In slum areas where absentee landlords own a great number of houses for the sole purpose of making money, great abuses occur. The tenement areas of any of our larger cities are a perfect example of this fact. So many other evils of urban poverty are caused by poor living conditions.

Evening the odds

Given the evil of urban poverty housing, where does law fit in? Can Urban Law help? The answer is yes, if we do not expect the impossible. Abuse of tenants is always possible in private housing because of the profit motive. As long as private landlords are permitted to gouge tenants, abuses will occur. It would be nice if the government could legislate absolute fairness in this area. Short of a police state, it cannot. Given the endless variety of types of houses and circumstances surrounding living in them, it would be beyond even the most advanced computer to legislate fairness. Any general rule would need an immediate, endless stream of exceptions. In addition and far more importantly, it would destroy free choice and the free enterprise system. The laws passed and adminis-tered by the government attempt to protect the tenants without unduly hampering the landlord. This is done because our society has a fundamental interest in seeing that all its citizens have liberty. Part of this fundamental guarantee of liberty is that a man has the right to live like a human being and not like an animal. It is this right to truly human life that permits the government to enact legislation in order to force private landlords to provide for their tenants living quarters which at least are habitable. *Javins* v. *First National Realty Corp.* is the most important case to date, affirming this principle. This means that habitable housing must be available at a cost that is not totally prohibitive. Within this broad framework of decent, reasonably priced housing, the tenant of a private landlord must work out a solution to the problem of the oppressive unjust landlord. Six major alternatives are open to the tenant in his program of combatting the slum landlord. They are criminal prosecution, failure to pay rent, abandonment of the building, receivership, rent control, and personal injury suit. Let us examine each in detail.

Seemingly the easiest method of forcing a landlord to provide the habitable housing that the law demands is to start *criminal prosecution* against him if he fails to do so. As with most sure-fire remedies, this one has more holes in it than can be seen at first blush. It is not that there is any question of the state's right to enact criminal laws to guarantee habitable housing. Previous discussion has highlighted the fundamental right of society to protect its members. Part of this burden of protection assumed by the state is that living accommodations will be habitable. From this it follows that it is a violation of the rights of individual citizens as members of society to be denied the right to habitable living. It follows as well that if the denial of an individual's right to adequate housing is serious enough, a penalty of criminal punishment will be merited.

The problem occurs not with the legality of criminal prosecution in housing matters, but in the difficulty of using this procedure effectively. Criminal prosecution of a landlord for providing seriously defective housing conditions means the state must be the prosecutor. Otherwise, it would be merely another civil action. Since the state is the prosecutor, it is necessary that the proper agency investigate the complaint and turn the matter over to whatever agency handles the criminal prosecution of this type of matter. This involves the tenant in the bureaucratic structure to a large degree. It encourages paternalism in that the tenant becomes highly dependent upon the governmental structure. If the government does not take action, the tenant is out of luck. In addition the tenant will not be helped by having the landlord placed in jail. No extra income will result to be used for necessary repairs. This is especially true while the landlord is sitting in a penal institution. Once he has served his sentence and is back on the street, the landlord will be in the foulest of moods and still will not have repaired the property. In addition, even if he does repair it, there is no payment to the tenant for past inconveniences and injury. Also, it is highly likely that the landlord will make an all-out attempt to raise the rent or evict the complaining tenant in order to make up the extra amount that had to be expended. In the long run, the tenant will probably still be the loser.

In addition to the unsatisfactory, long-range results that probably will occur if the state is successful in proving that the landlord broke the law, there is the added difficulty that it is extremely hard to obtain a criminal conviction in the housing area. The reason is that the guilt of the landlord must be proven "beyond a reasonable doubt" because this is a criminal case. However, the landlord has the ready-made, custom-fit defense that the tenant is at fault as well. This is a hard defense to get around in an area where any defense with some amount of truth submarines the prosecution charged with proving guilt beyond a "reasonable doubt." Given the fact that many who live in poverty come from different climates and cultures than the one in which they now live, it is not surprising that some of the fault for poor conditions is often shared by the tenant. Instruction by different community organizations on how to live properly in apartment houses can go a long way to remedy their lack of knowledge of household procedures. Even so, it would be hard to get around successfully the defense that it can be said beyond a reasonable doubt that the tenant is not in some measure at fault for the uninhabitable living conditions in the apartment. On reflection, criminal prosecution of landlords does not appear to be a good method for remedying severe housing violations.

A second method sometimes applied to try to clear up inhuman housing conditions is to *withhold payment of rent*. This is a dangerous method because it is a clear violation of the rental contract. This violation is an action that could give the landlord an excuse to evict the tenant. Poverty tenants clearly are the least able to find other satisfactory housing. Because of this it is absolutely necessary that withholding of rent be done properly. Otherwise the tenant is liable to be out on the street but quick. This is doubly true if the tenant does not have a lease, but is living on a month-to-month tenancy or as a tenant at will. Such tenants are on the shakiest of grounds even under the best of circumstances.

The theory behind a tenant's withholding all or part of the rent is that it will force the landlord to repair the apartment. When he fixes the apartment, the landlord will receive the money due on the rent. It cannot be emphasized too strongly that this method plays with fire. Unless done properly, the tenant involved is in the unenviable position of being a contract breaker who can be dispossessed at the whim of the landlord.

Legal help is badly needed when rent withholding is contemplated. Some say that the chances of success are greatly increased if a whole group of tenants get together to withhold all or part of their due rent until objectionable conditions have been fixed. Organizations of tenants have great possibilities in the field of progressive legal remedies during the 1970s. However, it must be kept in mind that tenant organizations and the devices they employ cannot be turned justifiably into weapons of extortion against landlords. It also should be remembered that a strong action against a landlord will almost definitely draw an equally strong response. This might not happen if the rent withholding or the like were done by a single individual since he would pose less of a threat. Before tenants man the barricades, they should think of the enormous demand for housing in all large cities and ask themselves whether the landlord could throw them all out and fill his house again immediately. In most cities, he could. If this is so, the stakes become very high if the tenants' association loses.

Social activism of this type cannot be permitted to obscure the fact that the landlord involved, no matter how reprehensible, is also a United States citizen. Since the landlord is a citizen, he has rights as well. Outsiders without a direct interest in the landlord-tenant controversy should tiptoe softly and be very careful of their involvement. An outsider without a justifiable legal interest in the case stands liable to a civil suit from the landlord for interference with the contract between the landlord and tenant. If the landlord is successful, he can collect monetary damages from the outsider. Alternately and more seriously, an outsider holding funds that are claimed as rent by the landlord could be exposing himself to a criminal charge of larceny for depriving the landlord of money that rightfully belongs to him. As we all know, one found guilty of larceny can be sentenced to jail. All community organizers and social workers who get involved in plans to withhold funds must realize that strong risk is involved in this situation. Should the outsider guess wrong and assist in a rent-withholding scheme in a case in which it can be shown in court that the landlord did provide habitable housing as specified in the contract, an outsider is in real hot water.

On the brighter side, if the landlord cannot demonstrate that he provided habitable housing, he has broken his contract with the tenant; or in the case of a month-to-month tenancy or tenancy at will, he has violated the unspoken promise that he will provide habitable housing. Since the landlord has broken his contract wholly or partially, the tenant is excused from payment wholly or partially. Since this is so, and to this degree, the tenant is not obligated to pay the landlord and consequently he is free to give that money to anyone he wishes. The outsider who involves himself in this type of case had better be correct in his judgment that the landlord has broken his contract so as to justify the nonpayment of rent to the landlord by the tenant. As we have seen, if the outsider is wrong, he can be penalized heavily.

The proper method to withhold or postpone payment of rent is to involve the court in the procedure. This is a protection that will shield the tenant and still have the desired effect of leaving the landlord in a less powerful position than at present. If the court agrees to have its probation department act as stakeholder, the tenant is placed in a very favorable position since the landlord knows that he will get his money when he completes the repair. Another acceptable alternative can be to have a lawyer, all of whom are officers of the court, hold the funds. Again, this is a protection against improper handling by the holder and a plan for stability and regularity in this complicated area of rent withholding. Socially militant groups have been active in organizing and encouraging tenants to band together to demand changes in unfair housing contracts. Agencies in this field can, if they exercise proper responsibility and judgment, be a significant force in bringing about social justice in our country. If they act irresponsibly, the leaders could be guilty of larceny and extortion. Lofty motives do not in a democracy excuse criminal conduct as a means to obtaining the sought-after end. Stability in a society demands that all good citizens follow the law. When one makes his own law, he starts a treadmill. Success in disrupting order for a good purpose can swiftly turn into disruption for a less good purpose and so on down the road toward a police state. Democracy will last only as long as the remedy to an unjust law is obtained by changing the law through recognized means and not disrupting or overthrowing the government.

The third major remedy for a wronged tenant is to *move out of his present quarters and live elsewhere*. This should not be shrugged off as a remedy. Many times tenants could find better housing if they really looked. Community organizers and social workers can help by encouraging tenants to look for alternatives to their present situation. Naturally, these agency employees can help investigate other housing opportunities in the area and also seek added taxpayer funds for public and nonprofit housing. In the same vein, fair housing legislation should be enforced conscientiously. The days when a person who can afford to pay more must surrender himself to poor housing because his race prevents him from obtaining the better housing that he desires should be over. Federal housing legislation blocks racial discrimination in virtually all private housing and provides strong teeth to back up this legislation. Considerate dealings by agency personnel with those tenants afflicted by inadequate housing can also overcome other objections they might have to moving. There is something about the habit of living in the old neighborhood that is hard to break. However, this type of attachment should not be allowed to dominate one to a point where unscrupulous landlords can get away with anything they wish because the neighborhood attachment of the tenant rivets him to his apartment no matter what.

There are negative considerations as well to the idea of moving. Leaving a house presumes that the new house to which one moves will be better. This is always a calculated gamble. As always happens, the one who made the suggestion will be turned upon if his advice proves to be bad. Another objection to this is that the guilty landlord is not punished or substantially inconvenienced. The present demand for housing makes this a sad fact of life. At the present time, he will always be able to get a new tenant as a replacement. To a large extent, the ultimate answer must come from effective housing legislation and further public and limited profit housing.

Receivership is the fourth remedy. It has many similarities to our second remedy, rent withholding. Both remedies hope to persuade the landlord to plow back into the building a sufficient amount of profits to insure that the building is made habitable. Even more than in rent-withholding cases, receivership is closely connected with court process and supervision. A receiver is someone appointed by the court to accept the rent owed to the landlord by the tenant. The receiver is charged by the court with taking the rent money and using it to hire and supervise workers for the purpose of making the house in question habitable. In legal terms, this priority for making repairs is called a "lien." A lien is a court-enforced legal designation of the order in which a certain sum of money will be spent. Liens become very important in all bankruptcy cases since there is not enough money available to pay everyone who has a justifiable claim against the debtor. It is imperative to get your claim to the head of the line. A similar situation exists in a rent-receivership case. The landlord will not get his rent money from the tenant until the receiver-supervised repairs have been made. As with every other so-called remedy, receivership is not as appealing as it might seem at first glance.

The most apparent objection to rent receivership is that the tenant seeking receivership will have to rely heavily on the governmental structure. This heavy dependence upon courts and government agencies carries with it guaranteed governmental inefficiency and red tape. Psychologically it is not good for a tenant to have no power himself, to be totally dependent upon the government and its courts for the basic guarantee of habitable living. An American citizen should not be placed in such an unenviable position.

Slums are good business for all but the tenant. It may not be apparent at first glance, but it is so. Landlords who lack any sort of social consciousness soon catch on to the fact that a lot of money can be made by charging high rents and providing little or no value and service for the tenants' money. This easy money acts like gold fever. Once the bug has struck, it is virtually impossible to shake. The desire to acquire more property in order to charge even higher rents and make even more easy money is overpowering. Soon the greedy slumlord runs out of money to buy even more tenements. Enter the banks! The banks provide mortgage money to slumlords in great amounts. This is one of the largest sources of bank income since the landlord-mortgagee must repay at a high rate of interest. This interest repayment is taken from the rents paid by the tenant. It is a foolproof system for both the landlord and the bank as long as the rent money of the tenant is available for this purpose. When a receiver steps in and takes the rent money of the tenant to pay for repairs required to make the apartment habitable, both the bank and the landlord get hurt. The bank may be affected directly. If the repairs to the tenant's apartment use up all the money available, the bank which is second in line gets nothing. This means that the landlord will not be able to pay off his indebtedness to the bank, and will lose the property to the bank. Since we are dealing with disreputable property which will need a great deal of repairs to make it habitable, it is unlikely that the bank will make a profit if it tries to become a landlord. It is easy to see why banks do not shout with joy when a legally appointed receiver enters the housing picture.

Even if the bank is lucky enough to get its money in this situation, it still stands to be the ultimate loser. This will occur because the slumlord who is third in line will lose his desire to buy more property. Why should a slumlord buy more property if all he does is to make money for the bank and the repair companies hired by the receiver? Therefore, the bank loses any time a receiver steps in. Either the bank will not get the money it is owed or, alternately, landlords will not borrow more money from the banks. It would be wrong to put too much blame on banks. Many times they have been helpful in financing new low-income housing and helping tenants. Still, there is at least the possibility that banks know that run-down tenements can be good business.

The fifth remedy to substandard housing is *rent control*. Ceilings on the percentage amount of rent increases can be fixed only by legislative action. This demands strong pressure on legislators. It is well to note that legislators are often lawyers and that lawyers have landlords and banks as clients far more than they do tenants. We hope the reader does not throw up his hands at this point and say what is the use. As with banks, legislators have many times preferred their constituent-tenants to their landlord-clients. Still, as with banks, the possibility of a conflict of interest occurs. This fact should be recognized and kept in mind.

Rent control interferes severely with the process of supply and demand. It can work undeserved hardship on good landlords and it smacks of socialism and government control. Rent control does not afford a total answer by any means. It is repressive, static, and tends to lock in both the tenant and the landlord. The tenant will not leave to seek better living quarters and the landlord will not make enough money to fix up the apartments to any great degree, or stimulate the economy by making new purchases. One good effect of rent control is that a landlord will not be able to raise rents unfairly in order to gain back his losses caused by the necessity of fixing the apartments.

Personal injury suits by tenants

None of the remedies we have seen puts money in the tenant's pocket for past violations by the landlord. It seems unfair to permit the landlord to keep all the money that he made unjustly during the period in which he collected large amounts for less than habitable living quarters. Unlike all our other remedies, a *personal injury suit* by the tenant would seek money damages for past injuries. This remedy would be for past violations only. Unlike all the other remedies suggested, its goal is direct punishment of the landlord for harm that he already has committed. Repair of the apartment is another matter, and has no bearing on the outcome of personal injury suits. A personal injury suit in this area would be just like a victim of a beating suing for money damages as added compensation, in addition to any jail sentence imposed after a successful criminal prosecution.

If personal injury suits were allowed as compensation for forcing a tenant to live in uninhabitable conditions, the door would be open to make landlords toe the line. The reason for recovery would be something along the lines of a collection from the slumlord for intentional infliction of mental suffering upon the tenant. Collection of damages for personal injuries caused by infliction of mental injury has been looked upon suspiciously by the courts in a variety of areas. It is very hard to put a money damage amount on the mental suffering which the conduct of another has caused. Fraud could easily occur. Especially in a housing case, other defenses are also readily available to the landlord. One is that no one has to live in uninhabitable housing. There is no gun at the tenant's head. He can move any time he wants. If he doesn't, he accepts the terrible conditions. In addition, the landlord can fall back on his old standby that the objectionable conditions are, at least partially, the fault of the tenant. For this reason, it would be claimed by the landlord that the mental suffering is self-inflicted and should not be the basis for recovery. It does not seem as if a personal injury action for intentional infliction of mental suffering is going to provide an easy solution for the tenant, although a recent Oregon case has shown a willingness to consider such a case. Also there is always the fear that the landlord will try to evict the tenant for causing trouble. Many state legislatures have recognized this fact and have provided for laws to punish landlords who try to evict tenants who had used the methods we suggested to improve their living conditions. So far this type of suit has had little success in the courts and the tenant has lost his apartment and not received any money damages.

This chapter has been one large false hope. It is clear that the law has not provided any adequate remedy to punish slumlords. This is so because it is good business for a significant portion of our society to take active measures to deny other members of society a decent place to live. As long as this condition exists in the hearts of men, the law cannot be expected to provide the total solution. Since laws mirror the will of the people, the legal structure is blocked to the extent that a majority of the populace find it profitable, therefore acceptable, to deny to other citizens the right to adequate housing. Law cannot be expected singlehandedly to clean the dirty linen for all of society. If one is interested in a detailed, extremely well done study of the whole area of tenant and private landlord relations, he could do no better than to read the excellent article of Professor Sax in volume 65 of the *University of Michigan Law Review*.

There is no doubt that the courts recently have become more interested in protecting the rights of tenants. For example, a recent Washington, D.C., case allowed a tenant to recover damages from her landlord for being beaten and robbed in the hallway. She proved that fifteen years ago when she rented the apartment, the landlord hired watchmen and doormen to protect the tenants and now he didn't. The court ruled the later lack of care was responsible in part for the tenant's injury. The landlord was ordered to pay all her bills. This is a very strong case, possibly too strong. However, it is an indication that courts are rethinking their ideas of fairness in the whole housing area. The name of this interesting case decided by the Washington, D.C., Court of Appeals in 1970 is *Kline* v. *1500 Massachusetts Avenue Apartment Corporation*.

Uninhabitable housing is being recognized as a disgrace in a land of opportunity for all. The proof of this national concern is displayed in the nationwide demand for meaningful federal and state housing laws and programs. More than anything else, this type of concern will serve to minimize the problem with slumlords. It is because an economic condition exists in which there are far more people than houses that the slumlord can prosper. It is a seller's market since the demand for housing is greater than the supply. This is generally true in all housing, but is particularly true for the poor. As the more wealthy are forced to take a step down in neighborhood location from what they desire, they gobble up, ordinarily at inflated prices, the only respectable housing that is left. Under ordinary circumstances this housing would be open to the poor. This leaves the poor with the scraps and at the inflated prices caused by the heavy demand of the well-to-do.

Only the insistence of the socially minded populace can reverse this situation. If public demand forces the government to give top monetary priority to building inexpensive, low-cost housing either directly or through substantial aid for nonprofit or limited-profit corporations, there is a possibility of a solution. If the alternative of low-cost public housing is open to the poor, the seller's market for the private landlord vanishes. It becomes a whole new ballgame. To attract customers, the private landlord will have to provide adequate housing at reasonable rent. With government money and brains, private housing can be transferred from a seller's market to a buyer's market. This would be far fairer than the present system and would be more in keeping with a free enterprise system. Since the problem basically is economic, the solution must be as well.

Public housing

The failures of public housing in many ways share great similarities to those of private housing. At least presumably the city or state is more interested in giving the tenants adequate housing for their rent. In practice, you sometimes wonder. The worst of bad city housing has to be seen to be believed. Added to all the other problems, nothing is more depressing than rows and rows of absolutely identical apartment houses. The main problem in public housing has been money. Cities that have put up public housing usually have done so on a shoestring, and often both the builders and the city employees involved have displayed less initiative and motivation than is justifiable. Loans taken out by the government to build the projects have to be paid back before necessary repairs can be made. The federal government will have to introduce added large amounts of money and efficiency to make good public housing a viable reality.

The legal rights of public housing tenants differ from that of private housing tenants because the right of a private landlord to operate within the free enterprise system is not carried over to public housing. The private landlord is free to contract with, dismiss, or retain any tenants that he chooses as long as he does not violate the race, religion, or creed provisions of appropriate federal and state housing acts. Since the government is no more than an extension of the people, it would be wrong to permit in public housing the arbitrariness in dealings allowed to the private landlord. Since the private landlord is primarily interested in making money, he should be allowed more maneuvering room than the state. The state is interested in serving the people, not in making money. Since all people are entitled to equal protection under the law, this equal protection must extend to housing tenants in public projects.

This equal protection aspect of public housing distinguishes it in many ways from private housing. The idea that a man can rent to anyone that he wants to so long as he does not violate antidiscrimination legislation, though true in private housing, is not so in public housing. Since public housing cannot be arbitrary the way a private landlord can be, a wholly different set of ground rules apply. Procedures must be erected to eliminate unfairness in selecting those who will be allowed to live in public housing. Arbitrariness will also be outlawed in public housing eviction procedures and in assignment to particular projects within a city on racial grounds.

The goal of lack of unfairness in public housing does not prevent the renting agency from setting up categories and criteria, but it does necessitate that these criteria be reasonable and contain at least the fundamentals of due process. Low-cost, nonprofit, or limited-profit corporation housing managed by groups of private individuals will fall somewhere between private and public housing regarding the relationship of owner and tenant. The basic idea of nonprofit or limited-profit corporation housing is a sound one; but the method of operation, especially the financial aspects, is yet to be resolved.

Summing up

The housing situation in this country, whether public or private, is still a fright for the poor. So much must be done; but if a simplification is permitted at this point, the main answer is to bring the supply up to or over the demand. At that point the lack of fairness in public housing will lessen, and the subtle devices of unscrupulous landlords who refuse to give leases and demand months of rent in advance, so that the landlord can enjoy the benefits of this money before he should be entitled to do so, will end. This is to say nothing of the physical defects that exist in private and public housing. To keep customers (at least in the private sector), these defects will have to end as well. How easy it is to say housing supply must equal housing demand. How hard in reality; how much effort, time, and money must be expended in this country in the 1970s to do so.

We are reaching the point in the book where we assume the reader understands what the law is. Now, he should start to get together with other interested urban poor. In numbers, there is strength. More workable ideas will occur and more legitimate pressure can be accumulated to encourage elected representatives to pass laws that protect the poor. When the poor realize it is in their best interests to work to have the government change bad laws and enforce good ones, Urban Law will be well on the way to success. There is no better place to start than in the landlord-tenant area.

Chapter 9

Our Divorce
Becomes Final Today

Setting the scene

The title for this chapter sounds like the title of a particularly sad, country-and-western song. Divorce is a very sad affair. It breaks up the basic fiber of society. Since they have little money to soften the blow, poor people are crippled more economically, if not emotionally, than are richer people by divorce.

The state becomes involved in divorce because of the great interest of society in the matter. Historically, nations of the Western world have developed a pattern of living that has the concept of marriage and family as its very core. Since the state is nothing more than the totality of all the people, it is made up almost exclusively of family members produced by another family and so on. The result is that our government is linked tightly to the concept of the family. Because of this fact, the state has a very strong interest in the legal effects of various relationships that come from the concept of the family. The most important are marriage, annulment, separation, and divorce. This is over and above the self-evident occurrences of birth and death.

The state takes a legitimate interest in the marriage relationship because marriage affects a great many areas of the law. The distribution of property, the ownership of bank accounts, the right to keep and raise children as your own, all hinge on the marriage relationship. In order to administer these areas in a fair manner, it is absolutely necessary for the state to know if the man and woman in question are married. The best way for the state to do this is to make the rules for the marriage relationship that must be followed. This is the reason why the state requires blood tests, proof of legal capacity to marriage, waiting periods, licensing clerics as chief witnesses, and all other conditions set by the state to be completed before a marriage is permitted.

Since you are not married unless the state says that you are, you cannot end a marriage unless the state says that it is ended. When the state declares a marriage ended, it is called a "divorce." We think of divorce as occurring on the day of the court decision; however, more technically the divorce takes effect a certain number of days afterwards. At this point, the divorce becomes final and irrevocable. It is important to keep in mind that legally the parties are not married until the state says so and not divorced until the state says so.

Annulments and separations

Two other legal terms that should be understood are *annulment* and *legal separation*. These two often become confused in the minds of many people and are used incorrectly as meaning the same thing as divorce. An *annulment* is an official declaration by the state that for some reason the ceremony that was an attempt at marriage did not result in a legally recognizable marriage. In other words, an annulment is an official statement by the state that no marriage ever took place. This differs from a divorce because in that case the state says that in the period between the marriage ceremony and the date that the divorce decree becomes final, this man and woman actually were married. A *legal separation*, on the other hand, is a court-approved agreement by the parties to a real marriage to live apart for a period of time under certain specified conditions while still technically remaining married to each other.

Before passing on to divorce, we should talk about annulments. Most people faced with the desire to end a marriage prefer an annulment rather than a divorce. The reason for this is easy to see. A person would much rather tell himself that no marriage took place rather than tell himself that a marriage did occur and was ended. At least psychologically, divorce indicates personal failure, whereas in some instances annulment indicates only a failure of circumstances without at the same time necessarily indicating personal failure.

Marriage is a contract in which two legally capable parties agree to join together in a permanent union. There is no marriage if the parties are not legally capable or if there is not really an agreement to marry. To be legally capable, it is necessary that both parties be of legal age to marry. States differ as to legal age, but usually there are three categories to be considered. The most common is an age over which people are free to marry without their parent's consent. As a rough rule this dividing line is eighteen. There is a second category that takes in younger people desiring marriage. It is necessary for them to receive the permission of their parents. If they do not, this marriage can be annulled up until the time the "younger party reaches the age of consent and ratifies the marriage at that point." This second category usually falls into an age limit around sixteen to eighteen. For teenie boppers of even less seniority, marriage is utterly void whether the parents do or do not give their permission. Of itself, no amount of consent or cohabitation can alter this reality.

In addition to age, marriages can be annulled for lack of legal capability if either party is not free to marry because of a previously existing valid marriage that has not been ended prior to the marriage in question. Other defects to legal capacity would be marrying a close relative or the impotency of either party or failure to pass the necessary blood tests.

The other essential element is consent. In the past there was more of a problem with forcing girls to be married against their will than there is today. Yet, circumstances could arise in which either party could claim successfully that force or undue influence was the main motivation for the marriage. If the required capacity and consent are present, the marriage is valid and can be terminated only by divorce or the death of one of the parties and not by annulment.

Marriages in trouble do not have to end in divorce. All who deal with these unfortunate people should try whenever possible to get the couple to get back together. Lawyers are faced with this duty when a client seeks a divorce. Clearly if there is any chance of obtaining a reconciliation, the lawyer should try to obtain it even though he will get less money for a few office visits than he would if he were to handle a full-blown divorce proceeding. It would be unethical if he did not make this humanitarian attempt to preserve the basic structure of society.

A legal separation is a possible alternative or part-way measure short of divorce. A legal separation occurs when either party goes into court to ask the judge for permission to live apart from their spouse. Generally this action is brought by the wife. If so, a support petition is usually attached to the separation documents in order to provide enough funds for the nonbreadwinning elements of the family to survive. The main advantage to a legal separation is that the parties live apart, but at least for the moment the marriage has not ended. Granted, it is clearly on the rocks. Still, there is the chance that absence will make the heart grow fonder. If the parties do decide to get back together, it is a relatively simple legal step to wipe out the separation agreement. On the other hand, if a divorce has been granted, it is necessary to go through another marriage ceremony. The chance of getting the marriage going again after a divorce is small because of the unpleasantness that necessarily goes along with these proceedings. The law is so much in favor of separation decrees instead of divorces that some states permit separation decrees in situations in which the husband and wife still reside together. This is not as silly as it sounds. If the husband who doesn't want to leave refuses to support a wife who has children and no money, separate support which is court-enforced may

be the only workable solution short of a divorce. Other circumstances which might permit living together while a separation
decree is in effect would be if the couple has no money but
a large house capable of division or if there were serious
illness on the part of either party.

In many cases, separate support is nothing but a fond hope.
Either or both parties has decided that it is definitely time
to move on to newer and presumably greener pastures. As
we all know, this decision often proves to be misguided. Yet,
once the wronged person makes up his mind and the lawyer
has explored all possible alternatives, it is best to give up
attempts to bring them back together and to attempt to represent the interest of the client as well as possible in the upcoming
divorce proceedings. To do this, it is best to keep bitterness
out of the picture as much as possible. Often this cannot
be done. Every lawyer who deals in this field regularly has
a stock group of stories of embarrassing events. Usually the
leading one is of a female client turning to her children and
saying, ''This is the nice man who is going to prevent daddy
from taking you to live with him.'' It is hard to prevent needless
and harmful emotional feelings from penetrating divorce cases.
The client will not be helped and his judgment may become
poor, leading to unfortunate decisions and impossible
demands at a time when clear judgment is desperately needed.

Divorce grounds

Divorce procedures are totally spelled out in state statutes.
This means that it is granted only in those cases in which
the law as written was followed. This means that to end a
marriage by divorce it is necessary to state and prove that
one of the causes recognized by the state as being sufficient
to end a marriage has occurred. Recently, these grounds have
opened up. It is interesting that as late in history as 1970,
Italy still did not recognize divorce for any reason. Some states
and countries still hold that adultery is the only reason that
will justify ending a marriage. Adultery is hard to prove for
obvious reasons. Also, using adultery as the only grounds fails

to take into account that many people are so desperate to end their lifetime promise that they will resort to private detectives, phony adultery raids, courtroom perjury, and other distasteful fictions to provide the necessary divorce grounds to satisfy the court even if adultery never did occur. For this reason states have loosened their divorce laws considerably. Today most states have a variety of reasons that will suffice to end a marriage. Seven different categories occur with great regularity.

Adultery is historically the most common. It is still thought of as the most seriously wrong action that a married person can do. It is a total rejection of the exclusivity that one contracts to observe in marriage. The trust and confidence that the working relation between man and wife brings about is ruptured often irreparably. Under the broader causes for divorce that are permitted these days, adultery is often not mentioned as a reason for the divorce even though it occurred. The reason for this is to save embarrassment and needless suffering. If the marriage is over, there is no point in adding more public bad feeling to that which exists already. This is especially true if there are children involved. An adultery contest invariably ends any realistic possibility of arranging custody and child-visiting arrangements that could be handled without bitterness.

There is nothing dishonest or illegal in failing to state that adultery is the reason for ending a marriage if alternate grounds exist as well. Any ground specified by the statute will do. Nothing is gained by alleging adultery if cruelty, incompatability, or desertion is available and can be used just as easily. Common sense must prevail. This is especially true in noncontested cases where custody, alimony, and property rights are the key questions.

In a divorce contest, adultery can be destroyed as a ground if it is demonstrated that the other party approved the adultery either by committing adultery herself or by having intercourse with the offending party after knowledge of his adultery. However, the offended party is permitted to attempt to fix up the marriage. Occasional acts of intercourse are permitted in this context and will not be considered as approval.

As a defense, the party charged with adultery merely has to deny that it occurred. On the authority of the older legal and practical maxim: "What is freely asserted, can be freely denied," denial by the party charged with adultery makes this a question of fact to be decided by the court. At this point, it is the obligation of the party charging adultery to prove that this act occurred. Since this is a civil case, the burden of proof is "mere preponderance of the evidence," and the party who must carry the burden is the party claiming that adultery took place. Naturally either party can be guilty of adultery, so the adultery of the other spouse can be used as a grounds by either party.

The second common ground for granting a divorce is *impotency*. This defect can be either physical or psychological in nature. The only pertinent question consists in an inquiry concerning the ability of the party in question to consummate sexual relations. Medical testimony is crucial in this area. If the impotency was present at the time of marriage and was not subsequently cured, annulment is a justifiable alternative to divorce. Impotency occurring at any time during marriage is grounds for divorce but not annulment since the party was potent at the time of the marriage. Impotency must be distinguished from sterility, which is the inability to produce children rather than the inability to have intercourse. Sterility is never valid grounds for divorce. As with adultery, the embarrassing nature of impotency testimony makes it better to use less personal grounds for a divorce proceeding if at all possible.

Desertion is the third ground available in most states to justify a divorce. Either party can be guilty and it is necessary that the abandonment of the marriage partner be total and continuous for a lengthy, specified period. Total abandonment has in mind an utter break. The abandoned spouse must not receive money from the other party. In addition, the abandoning party must not come back and live with the spouse either once in a while or even on rare occasions if the purpose is to have sexual intercourse with the partner. Obviously, this does not mean that the counting period must start all over if he comes over once a year to look at his bowling trophies. A little common sense must be observed. Periods from one to five years are the most common waiting periods before a divorce for desertion can be obtained. States vary as to the required length, but the period generally is substantial. The reason for this is to permit the parties to cool down, hopefully settle their differences, and get back together.

Alcoholism is the fourth common ground recognized by most states as sufficient to justify granting a divorce. Intoxication of this nature assumes that the problem be truly serious and continuous for a sufficient length of time. This is to prohibit a habitual "two beers before dinner" man or a man who gets smashed once from being cited for divorce as a common drunk. The law is more compassionate toward human weakness than that. Sad to say, many females are as susceptible to drinking liquor to excess as men; and the one whose drunkenness can provide cause for divorce can as easily be a female. It is logical to assume that drug addiction will be moving into this area as a separate grounds within short order. Addiction is such a problem that it is no longer proper to lump it under mental cruelty, although it certainly is cruel toward the nonaddicted party.

The fifth ground is *mental cruelty*, otherwise known as *cruel and abusive treatment*. This is a wide departure from the strict grounds required in the past. Every comedian has had numerous field days with jokes about mental cruelty. Everything from poor cooking to wife beating or even living with a disagreeable mother-in-law has sufficed on various occasions. Either party can use this ground. It is very hard to defend against and usually is not contested. Divorce lawyers assert that it is advisable as an alternative to adultery or impotency whenever possible.

A *substantial prison sentence for the other spouse* is another ground in most states. Five years is the most common requirement. It should be pointed out that it is the sentence pronounced by the judge and not the actual time served that is crucial. Therefore, even if a prisoner is sentenced to five years and is able to get out on parole in one year, he could still be divorced on the basis of a five-year imprisonment statute.

Nonsupport is the seventh ground usually permitted for divorce. Possible female liberationists would object to this, but women alone can use "nonsupport" as grounds for divorce. In some states this is lumped under desertion. Desertion is a serious situation that demands swift action from the court. If the case is drastic enough, the court may find it necessary to award the wife support from the husband's funds even before the case is decided. This is a rare remedy and its occurrence is usually limited to cases in which young children are involved.

Fortunately our society has not reached the point where the woman's role in bearing and raising children has been reduced to a neutral act deserving no special consideration from the state. With the drive toward limiting life by means of euthanasia, sterilization, birth control, and abortion, we may reach the point where a woman and mother are not favored by the law. This has not occurred so far. Consequently, even though a wife could earn money to support herself after a breakup, it has been held that this is the obligation of the husband in most cases. This is even more true if children are involved.

Not surprisingly, California has taken the American lead in legal casualness toward ending the marriage contract. As of the beginning of 1970, "incompatibility" has become an acceptable divorce reason in California. This is virtually impossible to disprove. The element of guilt has been removed from the California divorce law. No longer is it necessary to prove the fault of the other party. A neutral, fatalistic assertion that "we could not cut it together" will do. This should open up the support and alimony laws of California as well. The California approach has the merit of ending the seemingly endless battles concerning which party was at fault. Implicitly this recognizes the fact that just as "it takes two to tango," it also takes two to break or make a marriage. Negatively, the incompatibility ground chips at the bedrock of society. In a day when marital permanence and stability are threatened, this law seems to demonstrate a very casual governmental approach toward marriage that contradicts the fundamental historical, psychological, and sociological preference toward marriage in our nation.

Residence, support, and custody

States differ as to the length of time necessary for procuring a divorce. The difficulty of grounds needed to prove a divorce can also be a factor. The more casual states move divorces through at a far faster pace. The speed factor has led to problems in this area. Since each state has jurisdiction over marriages taking place between its residents or within its borders, it has just as much interest in the dissolution of marriages that took place within its borders or between its residents. Although a state will permit a marriage between nonresidents, it will not grant a divorce unless one party resides presently in the divorcing state or the parties were married in that state. Requirements of this type guarantee that the state in question will have a substantial interest in the serious matter with which it is dealing. This divorce contest becomes doubly serious when property rights and custody of children are being adjudicated.

The concept of residence becomes crucial in the divorce area. It cannot be so flimsy a requirement that the state in which the nondivorcing party resides refuses to observe the decision of the state granting the divorce. Mexico and Alabama used to have twenty-four-hour residency requirements for divorce. Since Mexico is not a state of the United States, there is no obligation to respect what it says in a matrimonial action as being binding in the United States. Most states will ignore a divorce decree or a property or custody award made by a Mexican court. Until Alabama changed its residency law a few years ago, many states refused to honor its decrees or awards either. On the other hand, in a state like Nevada six weeks will suffice for residence. This is why it is so popular as a divorce mill. Since six weeks is short, but legitimate, any support or custody decrees arrived at by a Nevada court will be recognized by all other states as long as the other party has notice that the other party has started a Nevada action for divorce. The immediate reaction of the party who receives notice that it is being divorced in Nevada is to run to its own local court and either get a divorce in the meantime (which means the local court will decide the property and custody rights) or more probably, since Nevada divorces are about the quickest around, obtain an order for separate support from the local court. This will tie the hands of the Nevada court and generally bring about a legal stalemate that will force both parties to arrive at a mutually satisfactory conclusion.

The rules for obtaining a divorce differ from jurisdiction to jurisdiction. However, they all have in common the requirement of "due process." This is true since substantial rights of people are being decided. Because of the requirement of notice to satisfy the fundamentals of due process, it is necessary to have legal methods of giving notice to the other party to the action that a divorce is being initiated and that they have the right to come in and contest it. The requirements as to adequate notice before a court hearing can be held differ from state to state, but are enough in common that it is safe to say as a general norm that three to six months is the normal time that must occur before a divorce petition is decided. In most states, there is a further period of time that must run after the decision before the divorce becomes final. Ninety days is a common requirement. At the end of that time, the divorce would become final automatically without any further action being needed. The advantage to this procedure is that it gives the party who brought the divorce action the time for "a second look" and an opportunity to call the divorce off if a change of mind had occurred in the meantime.

States truly interested in the permanence of marriage retain the same type of waiting period (thirty days, waiveable at the judge's discretion is most common) between the date that the parties stop living together as man and wife and the date that the divorce proceeding can be filed. As with a time lag before finalization of a divorce, the time lag between breakup and the start of the divorce action is thought of hopefully as a time period during which the parties will settle their differences and resume living together. In many instances, this is a fond hope; but at this point, the marriage is virtually over, so there is little to lose by this last ditch attempt at reconciliation.

Why are divorces contested? Originally for two reasons. Either to block a new marriage by the spouse who sought a divorce, or alternately to contest support or custody demands. Today, with a breakdown of the concept of guilt and fault, neither reason has as much legal validity. Divorce grounds have become so wide that anyone can find some evidence to support a sufficient ground in some state. Also, courts have become "liberated" to a point where courts sometimes have found it preferable to award child custody to women guilty of adultery. The waste of time in trying to contest a divorce becomes more pronounced when grounds as weak as California's "incompatibility" are considered sufficient.

Since contests are losing their effectiveness in divorce proceedings, consent and agreement have become the watchwords. Since we have arrived at the stage where in some states it is virtually impossible to attempt to block the granting of a divorce, the matters of support and custody have acceded to a higher priority. If the parties cannot agree on these arrangements, it will have to be left to the judge. Often, this is not satisfactory. If the disagreement between the parties was so severe that they were unable to reach agreement on a simple business arrangement, it is highly unlikely that the decision of the judge will receive any greater approval. Parties to a divorce are usually not in a mood to accept third-party suggested compromises. Whenever possible, they should agree among themselves with the assistance of counsel as to the division of the property associated with the marriage relationship.

The first matter for agreement pertains to custody of children. Ordinarily the mother is ready to assume this obligation. Custody of children has been granted to the mother even when, in some cases, she has been guilty of an adulterous relationship.

This is so because the measuring stick employed by courts dealing with custody cases is: "What arrangement is in the best interests of the child?" Under this line of reasoning, a court could find conceivable that it would be better for the children to be with an adulterous mother than with a negligent husband. It would be well if the parties could agree on this matter and the equally tricky problem of visitation rights. Courts rarely would disturb an arrangement with which both parties are happy.

As to financial arrangements for alimony, it is better also if the parties can agree. Judges can review these agreements, but rarely do they change them. A wife can testify, if necessary, as to the amount of alimony she needs to live in the manner to which she was accustomed and the husband can afford. A wife can waive alimony or take the settlement in one lump-sum payment. If she does so, she waives her right to go back into court and seek more. A divorced woman who remarries automatically gives up her right to any further alimony at the time of the remarriage. Until recently, husbands who were divorced by the wife were never entitled to alimony. Now if the wife is much richer than the husband, it is possible in a few states. If the husband's financial resources take a jump, the ex-wife presently receiving alimony can go back into court and seek an additional amount of money. This "changed circumstances" rule is a thorn in the side of a particularly cruel lot of young doctors and lawyers who marry a girl while they are both in college and then use her as a meal ticket through professional school, but divorce her when they graduate and are able to haul in the big money. The "changed circumstances" rule will provide these victimized women with some reward for their efforts and sacrifices.

The divorce hearing itself can be a source of tension. That is why all efforts are made to keep it as calm as possible. If there is not to be a contest on the issue of divorce, but only as to support, it would be hoped that the party being divorced would absent himself from the courtroom unless an issue came into controversy. The attorney for the party being divorced could notify his client that a question has arisen. It should be kept in mind that conversations between husbands and wives that are not witnessed by a third party are privileged. This means that neither one can testify in court as to private conversations with the spouse. In addition, discussions between a doctor and his patient, or a lawyer and his client, or a priest and his penitent, and in some locations either a social worker and his client, or a psychotherapist and and his client are privileged and cannot be introduced as courtroom evidence without the permission of the client. These provisions protect the sanctity of the relationships involved; and in the long run, the benefits of the prohibitions far exceed the small gains in information that disclosure of these secrets would involve.

The other major area for settlement in connection with the breakup of a marriage deals with property disposition. Again, compassion and detachment are the watchwords. Any radical breakup is a desperate measure. This is especially true when what is being split up is property that two people each thought of as being their own. A general rule of thumb is that the wife takes everything that the husband does not specifically claim. As to things they both want, arbitration must occur. One exception to this general rule is that in some states wedding gifts go to the spouse whose friend gave the gift. Under this rule, the husband would get the silver service contributed by his friend and the wife would get the men's golf clubs donated by her friend. Sentiment rules over practicality when dealing with wedding presents. In the case of land and housing, it is generally given to the wife because she would be more able to maintain it. Naturally an adjustment in other categories will have to be made in favor of the husband to give him his fair share.

Summing up

There is nothing noble or uplifting about divorce. It shatters what was designed as a permanent arrangement. The social disaster of divorce outweighs the legal problems. Still, the law has its own problems and finds this a difficult area. As with addiction to drugs and many types of crime, it would be a far more pleasant world if divorce did not exist. However, it does and must be reckoned with. In poverty areas where little money is available, a divorce may be the same thing as a one-way ticket to the welfare line for the deserted wife. This is especially true if she does have children to raise. The terribly inadequate day-care efforts started by the government do little to solve the problem. A major change in policy would be needed to permit deserted mothers to work. Even so, the problems suffered by divorced people should be a warning to others that they can unwillingly arrive in the same situation. "Marry in haste, repent at leisure" can be so true.

The terrible troubles of a divorced wife are easy to see especially when she has children. From a position of dependence upon a husband, she is suddenly thrust into the role of a provider. With other mouths to feed, this can destroy her life effectively. The husband will suffer as well since any chance he has to get ahead in the world can be totally blocked by the necessity of handing over a large portion of his paycheck to support a previous wife and children. All the way around, divorce is bad business for anyone, and fatal for the urban poor.

Chapter 10

The Big It and the Little Me

Setting the scene

Some people might think it a waste of time to spend a chapter on the details of corporate life in America. They are wrong for two reasons. First of all, we all buy from, and many of us work for, corporations. To receive a fair deal from them, we must understand them and know how to use them. Secondly, nonprofit corporations, if used properly, are the greatest weapon available for the poor to obtain the assistance necessary to bring about improvements in their life and working conditions.

Corporations are a way of life in this country. There is no way to escape them. The television sets we all watch were made by large corporations. The programs that we look at on these sets are presented by other corporations. The long, loud, endless commercials are paid for by many other corporations. All day long in everything we do, we are surrounded by and utterly dependent upon thousands of corporations. There is no way to avoid them. It is senseless to try. The size and power of these faceless giants make them mysterious and forbidding to all. They are doubly so to the urban poor. Often these people are employed by one of these large corpora-

151

tions in a degrading, impersonal way, doing an uninteresting, repetitive task. On the other hand, large corporations take back with greedy gulps what they have passed out. Given the basic fact of corporations, the urban poor should understand what they are and how they can be of help to him in his everyday city life. Don't just be used by them, use them yourself!

When we discussed the expanding circle of rights in America, it became clear that corporations have long enjoyed a favored place in our society. Since a corporation lives on past the death of its owners, the shareholders, it is easy to see that there is a distinct, clear separation between the corporation itself and those who run it. Although this is quite clear, it is just as true that it is humans who run a corporation. The only way to make a corporation act is through affecting those who manage the corporation.

Corporations are statutory creatures. Since they are artificial, they can exist only when the state says that they can exist. Once organized, a corporation goes on forever unless it voluntarily break up, runs out of money, or a time limit for its existence fixed by its articles of incorporation ends. To exist originally, and to stay in existence, it is necessary to follow the rules of the state. Although the rules vary from state to state, in general all states require that a group of men known as "incorporators" start the corporation. Generally the only requirement for incorporators is that they be three or more natural persons (i.e., not a corporation) over twenty-one years of age. Organizational meetings must be held to draw up and pass upon the certificate of incorporation and the by-laws. The certificate of incorporation (also called the "charter") is the formal document that establishes the corporation. The by-laws accompany the certificate of incorporation and specify the method in which the corporation will be run. These by-laws cover such matters as the number, length of term, time of meetings, and election of board of directors as well as the powers and duties of the directors and officers of the corporation. Once the certificate of incorporation is adopted, it must be submitted to and approved by the certifying official for the state, generally the Secretary of State.

In corporations formed for profit, the stockholders are the controlling force in theory. It is their money that enables the corporation to operate. It is for this purpose that corporations sell stock. A shareholder's interest in the corporation is represented by transferable certificates. It is these certificates that we commonly call "stock." Stock can be bought, sold, or borrowed upon just like a washing machine. Although it is all well and good to say that the stockholders run the corporation, this becomes rather ridiculous in the case of a very large corporation in which thousands and sometimes millions of shares of stock are outstanding. No one shareholder could swing the balance. In practice, what happens is that a small group of large shareholders get control and hold on by electing members of the board of directors who are sympathetic to their viewpoints. It is the directors who handle the overall management of the corporation. The directors in turn appoint the officers whose duties are to handle the day-by-day operation of the corporation. If the shareholders are dissatisfied with either the directors or the officers, the proper method to change the situation is to elect a new slate of directors who will in turn appoint new officers. Naturally this demands adequate votes to do so. The exact method of manipulating control is contained in the by-laws of the company.

Since a corporation is a person, it has virtually all the powers and business rights possessed by an individual person. Just like a natural, individual person, a corporation with the permission of its board of directors can sue another corporation or a natural person if injury has been done to it. This right to sue would occur among other times if an individual damages or steals the property of the corporation or fails to fulfill his contract with the corporation by not paying his bills. In an opposite manner, a corporation can be sued for any injury it causes to another just as if the corporation were a natural person. A corporation can buy, sell, or lease property as long as it is in keeping with the reasons why it was formed. In addition, it can make donations, carry on a business, pay pensions, carry insurance for its employees, and numerous other things that an individual in business could do. The main difference is that all natural persons die, whereas a corporation rolls mercilessly on. Just like the great sports dynasties such as the New York Yankees, the Green Bay Packers, the Boston Celtics, or the Montreal Canadians, individuals may fade out of sight, but new personnel are added to a corporation who are, many times, as good as, if not better than, the persons whose place they take.

Nonprofit corporations

Now that we know in general what corporations are, we can appreciate better the fact that they fall into three large categories. The first group is composed of *corporations organized for profit*. These are the most common and are that we call "private enterprise." Any group of men who link together to form a business for profit and receive state approval as a corporation are included in the category of being a private corporation. The second group of corporations are *nonprofit corporations*. These, as their name indicates, are formed for purposes other than to make money. Since ours is a profit-oriented and seeking society, ventures that do not seek money as their primary reward (i.e., nonprofit corporations) fall into certain general categories of a humanitarian nature. These categories include charitable corporations such as a nonprofit hospital or a home for the blind, a community antipoverty organization, the American Cancer Society; or educative corporations such as a college or library; or religious corporations such as a church or a religious order. The main difference between a nonprofit and a profit corporation is that the government gives up its right to collect taxes in the case of nonprofit corporations. The reason that the government does this is to encourage activities beneficial to mankind that otherwise would be unattractive because of the great financial risks involved.

There was the fear recently that the taxable exemptions

for nonprofit corporations would fall victim to the unquench-
able thirst for money needed by the government. Luckily the
United States Supreme Court calmed this fear in the 1970
Walz case. Writing for the seven-man majority, Chief Justice
Burger said that legislatures are justified in giving substantial
privileges such as an exemption from paying income tax to
nonprofit corporations as a "beneficial and stabilizing influence in community life." This preference or nonprofit corporations presumes two things. First, it is presumed that a nonprofit
corporation actually engages in business to fulfill its goal of
public service in a particular manner. This is not to say that
a nonprofit corporation cannot make money. Otherwise it
would not be able to produce the funds necessary to fulfill
its goal. However, there is a limit. Few people object to a
church taking a collection from its parishioners for funds. To
permit an activity such as the operation of a church to be
conducted without forcing it to pay taxes seems to be a
legitimate example of the "beneficial and stabilizing influence" provided by nonprofit corporations "in community
life." The same reasoning applies so as to permit extra tax
deductions for those individuals who contribute to these nonprofit corporations.

It seems highly questionable to allow a nonprofit corporation
to engage in what is commonly considered as a normal business enterprise even if the profits all go to the treasury of
the nonprofit corporation. To illustrate, it would seem to be
unfair for a church to run a grocery store free from taxes
in competition with a private grocery store that does have
to pay taxes. Participation in unrelated business in order to
raise funds lends questionability to the nonprofit corporation's
tax exempt status, at least as to the unrelated secular business
venture. To be specific, why should Rice University or the
Knights of Columbus, both former landlords of Yankee
Stadium, be able to hold it as an investment without paying
taxes, whereas for owning Yankee Stadium an insurance company or an investment holding company would be taxed heavily? This sort of activity by nonprofit corporations seems to
be a far cry from the main purpose for their existence. This

is not to say that a nonprofit corporation cannot engage in a normal business venture in order to obtain funds for its programs. However, if a corporation does choose to engage in a normal business venture in a substantial manner, it should submit to taxation as any other business would be expected to do. This interpretation should not be pushed to ridiculous extremes. A cake sale conducted annually by the "friends of the local library" poses little financial danger to a private business that sells cakes. However, when a university actively seeks to house conventions as a source of revenue or a church operates a publishing company that prints books on subjects ranging from herb cooking to defenses against no-trump contracts in bridge, we are in an entirely different situation. This is not a legitimate nontaxable way to raise money, but rather unethical opportunism that tends to cloud the many ethical fund-raising activities of nonprofit corporations, brings needless criticism, and takes away from their legitimate good works.

The second abuse to which nonprofit corporations easily can fall victim is engaging in political activity. Given the present-day climate of this country, the mere raising of this question discharges as much electricity as a high-voltage tension wire. It has been a familiar saying of constant validity in this country that there are three subjects that if you are wise you do not interfere with: another man's religion, his wife, or his politics. Observance of these rules has had many advantages in our history. They are undoubtedly a by-product of the rugged individualism of pioneer and colonial days. This respect for the rights of others and the respect for their freedom to disagree with our political or religious views are laudable objectives in theory. Yet, where has it gotten the Negro and the poor? Depending on your viewpoint of the inevitability of human suffering, the answer is everywhere or nowhere. If dissent is a mockery, the answer is to make it more meaningful. All this discussion presumes that democracy truly is the best form of government. Can true democracy be carried out by violence? The idea hardly seems possible.

Assuming that violence is excluded from the discussion and responsible dissent is really believed in as a positive function of the electorate in our nation, the question as to the proper way to dissent becomes important. Freedom of speech has guaranteed that any individual can speak out, march, politic for candidates, give campaign donations, and in general help any political candidate of his choosing or speak out on any issue of public concern. In the same manner as an individual, a profit-seeking corporation, through the medium of its shareholders and directors, can make political contributions within certain limits defined by the government. By paying taxes, the profit-seeking corporation has paid for the right to take a political stand. In this area, the artificial entity that is a profit-seeking corporation is in all ways like a natural person. However, since the nonprofit corporation is a drain on the state and because of its financial instability, it is a ward of the state in a very special manner.

Think of your favorite church. Could it exist in its present state if it were taxed like any other corporate entity? Probably not. Maintenance and improvements would suffer. Salaries for the clergymen and other employees would become a real concern. Consider the urgent pleas for funds today. Slice 40 percent to 50 percent of the profits off the top for taxes, and imagine the resultant tone of fund pleas. The same is true for universities and colleges. Costs have risen incredibly. Tuitions have tripled in some instances within a decade. In addition, government funds are an absolute must to finance research and building improvements. A crippling blow would be struck if 40 percent to 50 percent of the excess funds had to be sent to the government tax collector rather than to activate progressive steps in the educational programs and facilities of the university.

It should be clear to all that a truly nonprofit corporation should not be taxed. Is it ethical on the other hand for a nonprofit corporation to hide behind the government's financial protection on the one hand, and lash out at it with a club on the other hand because it disagrees with the politics of the government? It is clear from the process of reasoning employed by the author that he thinks not. Does this make those agents of nonprofit corporations who play both ends against the middle hypocritical and badly motivated? In most cases, probably not. It does not seem that they are shortsighted. Hypocrisy implies bad motives and generally these are not present in the attacks which those representing nonprofit corporations mount against the government.

Let us get away for a moment from the ethical considerations present in a nonprofit corporation entering into the sphere of politics. There is another side to the argument that we will discuss. This discussion applies as much to churches and community organizations as it does to colleges and universities and the theory is that it is bad business for a nonprofit corporation to pick sides in political controversies. The answer is as simple and as old as mankind. It is a part of human nature to take care of those who are nice to us. This applies just as much to government officials as to anyone else. In the long run, a politically oriented nonprofit corporation will get hurt. No administration lasts forever. During the thirties and forties many Republicans might have argued with this and thought that the Democrats would never surrender power, but Dwight Eisenhower came on the scene. Through assassins' bullets, a seeming Kennedy dynasty was cut short at its start. The point is that all trends end. The favored child will, at some point, fall from favor. Often this occurs at the time when it can least be afforded. By staying out of the poltiical ring, nonprofit corporations are less likely to be tossed around in the uncertain arena of political favor and popularity. A hands-off attitude toward political strife traditionally has marked the dealings of nonprofit corporations with the government. When nonprofit corporations stay out of politics, only the merits of aid for the particular corporation involved come into play. If politics are involved, the added questions of who is in power and who is not and how you have dealt with those politics in the past become of monumental interest. If partisan politics becomes a measuring stick for government grants to nonprofit corporations, the battleground will become bloody with these corporations going out of their way to win their case on a political rather than on an objective basis. With all their present problems, nonprofit corporations are needlessly injecting themselves into a hornets' nest if they become overly interested in partisan politics.

Those who disagree have sat patiently back waiting for the argumentation along the above line of reasoning to cease. At least it is hoped that they would sit back patiently. The other alternative, and it is a disquieting, frequently occurring one, is that bitter feelings will rise to the forefront and the popular, randomly applied charge of a "cop-out" will be hurled against the author. The impassioned rhetoric is a by-product of our times that must be borne with as much calmness and charity as possible. This does not mean that one convinced he is right must back down to a verbal onslaught. It is necessary that he listen and adjust his views if necessary. If not, he should work to find any common ground and hope that the other party will see the light as to the rest.

The standard argument other than that this is a cop-out is that this particular subject in controversy is too important an issue for the church, university, foundation, community organization, etc., to be quiet. It is a humanitarian issue, not a political one, is a variation of the same argument. Is there an absolute right for an American nonprofit corporation to intervene? This is a most difficult ethical question. Though hard for some to understand, the answer is no. This is not to say that John Jones, the minister; or John Jones, the community organizer, could not state his personal political opinion and band together with others of a like mind. This is an important concept which the emotions of the moment should not hide. Any individual, no matter what his position, pays taxes on his salary and is a voting citizen. As such he has the right, even the obligation, to speak out and organize to the degree that he feels necessary in order to have his political views prevail. Yet as discussed, a nonprofit corporation neither votes nor pays taxes; and it is wrong for individual citizens to utilize the revered status of a nonprofit corporation as a shield for their own political views. A nonprofit corporation is granted its status because it has a definite charitable, nonpolitical goal. When it drifts into politics as an institution and places its funds at the discretion of those interested in political activities, it has abused on its part the concept of a nonprofit corporation and deserves to be treated and taxed like any other corporation. To say the same thing another way, a community organization has enough to do fighting poverty in the neighborhood without trying to elect Democrats at the same time.

Public utilities

The third distinct type of corporation to which we have reference are those corporations qualifying as *public utilities*. This is a general term for those corporations that provide us with such essential services as light, water, power, and telephone service. When these public utilities were first organized, they were granted the privilege of being the only company of their kind in that area by the states in which they began to operate. Another way to describe this is to say that the public utility in question was granted monopolistic powers as to the service in question in the states where they would function. The states took the unusual step of granting monopolistic powers to these public utilities because it is necessary for the public utilities to run up enormous debts in order to pay for and maintain the expensive equipment needed to operate effectively. Because of this large outlay for expenses, chances of profit are small. If there were competition in the public utility fields, any chance of profit would be nonexistent and no one would purchase the stocks and bonds of the utility companies. For this reason, the utilities are allowed to operate in their area without competition.

Because the states grant the privilege of being a monopoly to the public utilities, they correspondingly retain a greater control over the business affairs of the public utilities than they do with other businesses incorporated in their state. This is to protect the public. Otherwise the public utilities could charge as high a price as they wished for providing their services. States regulate the rates and policies of the public utilities. This fact should be understood and kept in mind by the urban poor. If they have a complaint, the state or federal agency that supervises the utility in question should be told about it. Since public utilities operate with such governmental approval, the demands of "equal protection" weigh heavily on the shoulders of public utilities. It is the right of the urban poor to equal treatment by public utilities, and it is the duty of the states to enforce this right for all its citizens.

The telephone company is a perfect example of a public utility for us to employ in discussing this area. Unlike a federal agency, the telephone company has private shareholders. Its shares are for sale on the important stock exchanges. At their annual meeting, these shareholders elect the board of directors as is done in any profit-seeking corporation. However, unlike other profit-seeking corporations, a utility like the telephone company must receive permission from government agencies to set rates, add to their equipment, or make many other significant changes. Public utilities must be licensed by the government because of the necessity to use all land, whether public or private, to install their equipment. In order to be able to carry out this function, they have been granted the right to acquire land by eminent domain.

Public utility commissions that supervise these monster corporations cannot do everything. The utilities are so large that there is no way in which these regional monopolies can be regulated totally. The monopolistic arbitrariness often manifests itself in the ghettos. On the one hand, the utility has an obligation to its shareholders to earn as much of a profit as it can. On the other hand, it must be remembered that given our urban society, such essentials as heat, light, water, and phones are close to an aboslute necessity for life. Can a utility justifiably cut off anyone's heat if it is 20 degrees outside, or can it cut off the water if there is within a sick child? In these cases, at least temporarily the monetary picture seems unimportant. More has to be done to impress this fact on public utilities. Their policies can be a terrible imposition on the poor. Is their any justification for a multimillion dollar corporation depriving a poor person of the equivalent of a week's salary as security for a new phone or turning on the lights? What makes this sort of policy all the more infuriating in such a rich corporation is that downpayments have a habit of being collected with far more vigor in the poor urban areas than in the more well-to-do suburbs. This a clear disregard of the public service aspects that should be demanded of a monopoly whose guaranteed market is protected totally by the government. The need for the poor to pay larger downpayments and swift cut-offs for the poor are in conflict with the protection and service that the government and, by extension, its favorite sons, public utilities, should permit. The government through welfare departments and public service agencies must step into the picture and bring more equality and compassion to this area than has existed up to the present. It is about time that public utilities fulfilled their claim by protecting all the public.

Partnerships

The only form of multiple ownership of any importance that does not follow the corporate type of organization is a partnership. A *partnership* is an association of two or more persons joining together for the purpose of making a profit in carrying on a business. The differences between a corporation and a partnership are enormous in nature and of sufficient importance to be examined at length. The first and most important distinction is that a partnership is not a separate legal entity apart from the partners. This is opposite to the concept of a corporation, which is a separate legal entity. Since a partnership is not a separate entity, it is not possible for one partner to protect himself from legal liability for the misdoings of another (of course, we would never be guilty of misdoings or mistakes ourselves) the way that it is possible with a corporation. This means that each partner holds the real and personal property of the partnership as a tenant in common rather than having the property owned by the corporation of which a shareholder owns part. The big difference is that if a partnership is sued, there is no limitation of liability for the individual owners because the partnership is not a separate entity. Creditors are able to take all the property and assets of the partnership firm to satisfy debts that are outstanding. Since there is no separation between the partner and the partnership, the creditors can go after the separate nonpartnership property of any partner if the full amount of the firm debt cannot be satisfied from the firm assets. Since a corporation is a separate entity from the shareholders, this misfortune cannot occur to a shareholder of a corporation. Once the corporate assets and property are exhausted, the game is over. Unfortunately, this is not true for a partner in a partnership firm. A partner in a failed partnership can lose his house and everything else.

In a way, a partnership is like a marriage. The partners are bound to each other through better or worse for the length of time for which they agreed to operate a partnership firm. They can all make a fortune through the brilliance of any one of the partners since they all share in the profits. Alternately, since partners share all the losses, the incompetence or mistakes of one of the partners can ruin all. Unlike a corporation, a partnership cannot last forever. The death, insanity, or bankruptcy of any partner will terminate the partnership just as will the agreement of all the partners or the expiration of a time limit originally agreed upon for the duration of the partnership by all the members. There is no right of succession in the relatives of deceased partners unless provided for in the partnership agreement specifically. Many supposedly wonderful partners have turned into instant devils when the smell of extra money drowns out the responsibility and justice that they should feel toward the relatives of deceased partners.

One last nail in the coffin of partnerships is the area of taxation. Since a partnership is not a separate entity, the partners must pay taxes on all profits at the enormous individual tax rate. Corporations, as separate entities, are taxed at slightly less enormous rates. All in all, partnerships are a bad gamble for any sort of a going concern.

Corporate responsibility to the poor

Corporations are a way of life in this country to an amazing degree. American business is so large and widespread that Europe has fears that its home economy will become a satellite for American corporations operating on their soil. American corporations doing business in Europe in many ways are the second largest economy in the world. Internationally or locally, there is no way to avoid the pervasive influence of American corporations. A better question for the poor is, why bother? Return to our original statement that a corporation is a person, even though an artificial one. Since a profit-seeking corporation is a person, it should as a taxpayer be thought of as a citizen for our purposes. The corporation as a taxpayer-citizen cannot turn its face away from the suffering of the people living in ghettos. Just like a natural person, the corporation, artificial person though it may be, is as responsible as any other American person for the necessity of our saying that the United States will not be a real democracy until all Americans are free and provided with an equal opportunity.

Granted that there is a great deal of hot air and generalization in a call for corporate responsibility; it cannot be written off as this alone. The poor are customers of these corporations just as much as those with more money. Strictly from a business angle, an intensive campaign to upgrade urban living standards will help the corporations involved. A higher living standard can very well mean that formerly poor urban residents can buy more of the corporation's product. However, the motivation for corporate concern and activity should not rest merely on this monetary justification. Corporations share in American productivity and success. They have an ethical, moral, and professional obligation to the urban poor strictly because the urban poor are citizens of the same democracy as the corporation and, by extension, the owners of the corporation.

In the abstract, it is very easy to call for corporate responsibility. So often though, this call is justified because the corporation fails in this regard. Will further begging and pleas for goodwill do the trick? Probably not. Eventually the time must come when the vicitmized consumer will draw the line and try to rally his forces to prevent further exploitation. Advocates of this sort of activism must be sure that their cause is just and that their method of redress is legal. Otherwise, they become vigilantes and forfeit the right to our sympathy and assistance.

Again, we must emphasize that outside of the law there is not salvation, but only further anarchy and strife. If the law is unjust, change the law. Do not tear apart the legal bedrock of the whole system in order to effect change in some particular area.

The rights of consumers are being enhanced presently within the framework of our legal system. Legislators recognize the fact that some corporations do not deal in a fair manner with their consumers especially in the credit area. Legal steps are being taken to insure that those who do not have the money at hand to afford a purchase will not find it necessary to add on an enormous amount of extra debt in exchange for the privilege of payment over a period of time. A wise federal judge once observed: "Law does not define fraud since it needs no definition and is as old as falsehood and as versatile as human ingenuity." Nowhere is this statement more true than in the area of contracts for the extension of credit in consumer purchases. If the company extending credit intends to trick the customer as to the amount or percentage that he will have to pay for the privilege of charging his purchase, actual fraud occurs. However, even if the company extending credit does not intend to deceive the customer, if the agreement is so complicated and detailed that a reasonable man would be likely to misunderstand it, fraud can still occur. It is highly doubtful that anyone other than a lawyer could understand the terms of many credit agreements, and sad to say, it is doubtful if all of them could. Can the average citizen say he knows what he is doing? Undoubtedly not. This situation must be changed.

No area of the law is more confused than that of small claims court. Few lawyers and even fewer private citizens understand its workings. This is a shame. Small claims court is the one place where the average person can present his contractual claims and receive court assistance in enforcing his just claims usually without the necessity of going to the expense of hiring an attorney. Small claims court has as its only purpose: handling small money claims without the need of all the forms, details, and procedures that go into a regular trial. If you are given a defective storm window or the new stereo has a tinny sound or the landlord won't fix the furnace, the easiest remedy is to go to small claims court and seek a judgment in your favor.

Why don't the poor use small claims court? Many don't know about it; many are afraid to get involved in the legal machinery; and many don't realize the powers a court possesses to enforce its judgments. No two states have the same rules concerning small claims court. The maximum amount which you can demand in small claims court differs from state to state. Figures ranging from $400 to $1,000 are the most common. Most states permit the poor person to appear without an attorney. Almost all states require that one put up a filing fee. Rarely is it more than $5. If the other side does not come into court on the day it is summoned, the party who brought the case wins automatically. This often occurs. The court can enforce its orders by contempt or attachment, if necessary. Therefore small claims court is nothing with which to fool around. However, it can help the poor. Neighborhood agencies should instruct the poor in the proper methods to make it work to help them.

The federal government has taken recent, strong steps to protect the customer in this sort of situation. The law which was passed in 1968 is called the "Truth in Lending Law." All throughout its many sections and especially in the area known as "Regulation Z," this law, which has strong penalties to ensure its enforcement, demands that those businesses or services in the habit of giving credit to individual customers must spell out clearly in everyday language such essential facts as the cost of the product or service if paid for solely in cash; and also the exact cost of consumer financing charged in terms of annual rates. Other parts of the Truth in Lending Law prevent excessive attaching of wages, punish loan shark credit charges, erect a national commission to study consumer credit, and prevent misleading advertising of credit arrangements.

On the whole the Truth in Lending Law leaves to the individual states the responsibility for erecting its own laws as to the percentage charge for credit that is so high as to be illegal as usurious. The states either have their own special laws in this regard, or have adopted the Uniform Consumer Credit Code.

In addition to usury, most states have taken steps to protect customers who buy on credit in the situation in which the retailer demands that the customer make out a negotiable promissory note as a condition for receiving credit. The retailer than sells this negotiable note for cash to a finance company. Unfortunately all or part of the goods or services purchased by the customer turn out to be defective. Under traditional law, the customer was forced to keep paying to the finance company as the installments came due, even though the goods or services were defective. The only remedy available to the customer was to institute a separate suit against the retailer to recover for the defective goods or services. Naturally most of the retailers involved in this sort of situation are of less than the highest character and recovery against them could be very difficult. Legislators have seen the unfairness of this situation, and both statutes of various states and the Uniform Consumer Credit Code have taken steps to eliminate this inequity by various provisions making it illegal for the finance company to enforce payment by the customer when the retailer fails to live up to his part of the bargain.

Two other areas of potential difficulty for consumers, credit cards and deficiency judgments, are coming under close inspection these days. Legislation occurs frequently to limit the amount of loss a credit-card owner can suffer should his card be stolen and used by another. Similarly, legislation is occurring to prevent retailers and collection agencies from enforcing payment of questionable claims by threatening the complaining customer that they will fix it with credit rating companies so that he will not be able to receive any sort of credit from thereon. In a similar way, action is being taken to insure that credit agency reports are accurate and given out only to those with a legitimate reason for receiving them. As to deficiency judgments, especially as to automobiles and home mortgages, states are more and more coming to the conclusion that in a variety of situations repossession of the property in question is enough satisfaction from the seller if all expenses are satisfied. Anything over that is often blood money. Little is available and no one is aided to a great degree. It is best to close the books. A recent California statute [Cal. Code (iv. Proc. 1580b)] is an example of such a new and good law.

If the product that a consumer buys from a corporation is defective to such a degree that he is injured seriously, he is able to collect a substantial amount of damages. Suppose, however, the damage is small; the wheel falls off the tricycle or the sound in the stereo is slightly tinny. What can he do? Federal courts do not allow damage suits where the amount sought is less than $10,000. It is necessary to go to a state small claims court. If the manufacturer is not local, the customer may have a hard time collecting. An ideal solution that would prevent manufacturers from hiding behind slightly defective products in order to make an unjust profit would be "class actions." These are suits in which one or a few dissatisfied customers could sue on behalf of all the other customers dissatisfied with the product in question. Recovery would be split with all the other consumers whom the one or ones bringing the suit could locate. In "our tricycle with a defective wheel" example, any wronged consumer could sue on behalf of all the consumers who bought this type of tricycle that had a defective wheel. If there were 3,000 people who bought this type of bike and it was estimated that damages suffered by each was $10, a suit brought by one on behalf of all would have damage claim of $30,000 rather than $10 if the consumer had bought it for himself alone. The class action for $30,000 would be far more than the $10,000 amount needed to sue in the federal courts.

At present, federal courts and most state courts have strict requirements surrounding class actions. However, aroused consumers are demanding action beyond the type which federal agencies are able to provide. Legislators are beginning to propose legislation to help the consumer. The possible power of class actions can be illustrated by citing the example of a recent $427,500,000 suit brought by two pickup truck owners against a large motor company on behalf of themselves and 200,000 other owners of this company's trucks for a five-year period. The two bringing suit charged that the wheels were defective structurally. Some protection must be given to corporations in this area to see they are not vicitmized either. However, it is safe to say that class actions are a potent consumer weapon of the future.

Corporations have a lot of positive benefits. Our country would not have reached its present stage of success and prominence without them. However, though not alive, they must be held to a level of responsibility. If they are not, the poor are exploited. We have to look only as far as the National Advisory Commission on Civil Disorders (the Kerner Commission) for a warning as to the possible consequences if the poor are exploited by corporations. The Kerner Commission listed dishonest conduct in the marketplace and laws that permit or even encourage this as a most important cause for recent lawlessness. We cannot tolerate this lawlessness; but we cannot tolerate the dishonest marketplace dealings or laws that encourage it, either.

Activism in any area can be dangerous and can easily swing from a positive force to a negative one that tolerates no opposition, right or wrong, in its plunge toward its goal. In areas such as ecology, minority rights, products for defense-related industries, and ghetto franchising, there is the fear that the impersonal giant, the corporation, will be made the fall guy for every special-interest group that comes along. Granted many of these groups have valid causes. In fact, even with those groups that do have valid complaints, the large corporation is not always the proper target for their attack. Even so, there are many areas in which corporations could do better. Day-care centers are one crying example. Neighborhood health clinics could be provided for by the corporation. Low-cost housing projects could be financed by these corporations. If the basic commitment and interest is present, the possibilities for service are virtually limitless. A profit-seeking corporation is most sensitive to the opinions of its shareholders. Since most of the shareholders of large corporations are of medium-income class or better, the corporate commitment to the poor will necessarily mean for them at least a temporary drop in corporation profits. This in turn will mean a decrease in dividends to these middle-class or better shareholders. Their true commitment to ridding poverty will be tested where it really hurts, in their pocketbook.

Most of what has been said about the need for added efforts and responsibilities on the part of profit-seeking corporations applies to nonprofit corporations and public utility corporations as well. A nonprofit corporation can be stripped by the state of its tax-exempt status if it fails to live up to its humanitarian purposes. Possibly this would be the best weapon to be pursued by those groups and individuals truly interested in protecting the poor from exploitation. Petitions to the licensing authority, generally the Secretary of State, seeking to strip a nonprofit corporation of this status, would be very effective for two reasons, if successful. First of all, there is the obvious effect that the formerly tax-exempt corporation will have to pay large sums in taxes to the state and federal government as it well should if it fails to observe the rules to which it agreed when it applied for a tax-exempt status originally. Also true but less appreciated is the fact that would-be contributors cannot obtain a tax exemption for contributions to any theoretically nonprofit corporation that does not have a tax-exemption identification number. Tax exemption identification numbers are granted to true nonprofit corporations after a government investigation. Because of this fact, it is absolutely necessary that a nonprofit corporation do everything possible to keep its tax-exempt status. In some cases it would be necessary for the challenged corporation to define and follow its charitable, educational, or religious goals a little more closely if an attack were raised against its tax-exempt status.

The public utilities are regulated, but it seems that even more has to be done in this field. Because of their monopolistic power over the whole market in which they operate, the utilities resemble a federal agency in the amount of service extended to all the people. Since this is so, the due-process and equal-protection guarantees that all citizens possess when dealing with the government should be more closely observed by public utilities. Just as in the government's dealings with its citizens, there can be no differentiation between rich and poor as rich and poor; the same standard should be used by public utilities as well.

Summing up

In unity there is strength! Corporations have used this sort of approach to reach great heights of success in our country. This chapter has tried to point out that corporations are little more than groups of citizens joined together to run a business in a more efficient manner. They should be reminded that each of them has an obligation as an American citizen to be receptive to the needs of the poor. Therefore, by extension, this obligation is shared by corporations which are run and owned by American citizens.

The nonprofit corporation was covered in detail because it is the best possible agent for spreading Urban Law. Still, it must be used properly or the people will restrict its field of operation and privileges. As long as a nonprofit corporation sticks to the goals for which it is organized, it can go a long way toward solving urban poverty. Some areas in which non-profit corporations can have success will be looked at in the next chapter.

Chapter 11

Making Uncle Sam
a Real Uncle

Setting the scene

When "Uncle Sam" is mentioned, the World War II recruiting picture, which actually comes from the original drawn by Howard Chandler Christy in World War I days, is still the picture formed in many minds. The portrait of a stern-faced figure with a pointed, accusatory finger is hard to forget, as is the accompanying catch phrase: "Uncle Sam Wants You." Times have changed and today it should be the public pointing its finger at "Uncle Sam" and saying: "The Public Wants You, Uncle Sam." All citizens, but especially the poor, should feel no sense of bashfulness in this regard. After all, "Uncle Sam" to a large extent is no more than the sum total of our tax dollars. We have the right and the obligation to see that this tax money is spent properly. Granted that in such a large operation there is an inevitable mass of waste, nonetheless a large proportion of this money collected from the taxpaying people is spent wisely. Why then do not more of the benefits from this money filter down to the average citizen? The answer all too often is that the average citizen does not know that these federal programs exist, and that only a request is needed to put these available programs into operation for the benefit of those who ask for them.

The ignorance factor as to currently available government services is very high. At the same time, it is understandable. Government is one of our biggest businesses. We all know this is so. It has spread its claws into so many areas that it would be a major accomplishment for the average citizen merely to give the name and primary function of each cabinet member now in office. When one considers that each executive department of cabinet rank has a budget running to many millions of dollars annually, the impossibility of the average citizen being able to take advantage of all the various programs set up by the different departments becomes clear. The government is much too large and complex to have the time to tap the citizen on the shoulder and tell him which of its many services he needs. It is time for the citizen to tap the government on the shoulder in order to have it employ the available tools to help him. Too much is made of the need for new legislation to help the poor. Of course, this is a worthy project. Still, the fact remains that only the surface has been scratched in the employment of already funded programs. It is the main point of this chapter that at present it would be more profitable for the poor to make a study of what is already funded. Let us use what we have available first. It is so much easier to be funded from existing sources rather than seeking new sources for funds. In addition, so many of the new plans to help the poor are nothing more than reworkings and often just restatements of what already exists untapped and often unknown. Since all of the presently funded programs were in some form bills passed by Congress, this area deals with "laws" in their truest sense.

Using the local congressman

Where do the urban poor, either alone or through their nonprofit community organizations, start to tap this supposed gold mine of federal programs? The answer is their local congressman and his staff. The congressman has a double function.

He is charged with representing the people in his district in official Washington, just as much as he is with his function to study and then vote on current legislation. Too often the representative capacity is overlooked. This is silly when we consider that the name of the branch of Congress in which the congressman serves is called the House of Representatives. This is not to say that your congressman is the second messiah. Clearly he is not. Like every other citizen, the congressman can engage in certain types of legitimate conduct. Putting undue influence on the Executive is not one of them. However, it should be remembered that being a congressman is a nice job. If you doubt this, just examine how many candidates appear the next time when an opening occurs in your area. Everyone living in the district of the congressman knows a large group of voters. If the individual voter is pleased by his dealings with the congressman, he speakes well of him to his relatives and friends. This adds to the chance that those in this group who live in the same congressional district will vote for the congressman at the next election. If the voter's impression is unfavorable, it is just as likely that they all will vote against the congressman. Therefore, it is in the congressman's best interests to be of help to his voters. This reason is over and above the real likelihood that it was interest in genuine public service that brought the congressman to seek his position in the first place.

As stated, there are only so many things that a congressman can do for his voters. However, he can serve in the most important role of opening the door to the proper Executive department. The congressman or his staff has frequent dealings with the Executive. This is so because it is necessary for Congress to pass all money bills for the various Executive departments. So over and above the genuine spirit of public interest possessed by members of the Executive Branch, they know that if they do not keep Congress happy, they will not receive the money to bring their plans into operation. Therefore, an introduction from a congressman to the proper official in the particular Executive department in question will be appreciated and everything will be done to help the voter.

It is easy to become overly cynical. The news media are quick to assign less than totally flattering roles to government workers. Yet in the main, this is not true. They are just as hardworking and interested as anyone else. We believe in the efficiency, hard work, and dedication of such federal units as the F.B.I. and the Postal Service. Not to tear down the fine employees of these branches, but there is no reason that they should have received so much more recognition than any other branch. There are many other branches just as efficient and willing to please. All that they lack is the public image received by the F.B.I. and the Postal Service.

Useful government programs

The average person does not have the time or money to go to Washington to see his congressman or a member of his staff and make the rounds of the various Executive departments. Since this is so, the local office of the congressman should be used as should the regional offices of the various Executive departments. In addition to this, groups of the poor should band together to express their views and see that their needs are covered. Strong action on the part of private groups is a great help. However, the various federal and state-financed antipoverty agencies are a ready-made group for starting the wheels rolling to bring into their area the employees and programs of the government that are available. One of the great shames of agency practice is that too often they have not been able to see the forest for the trees. So many of the problems of the poor are connected that coordination is badly needed. So far it has not occurred in any appreciable amount. Most antipoverty agencies are so concerned with their own budget that they tend to lose sight of the fact that a combined project along with other government agencies and departments could be of vast help to all the people. Let us look at some of these programs presently existing and funded that could be of help to the poor. However, enough examples will be suggested so that one will have enough data to ask himself whether he or the agency with which he deals could be a lot more active in obtaining and benefitting from government programs.

Starting with the letter "A," we shall deal first with the *Department of Agriculture*. To the city dweller living in a project, it is more likely that he is exposed to rats than cows and sidewalk pavement rather than country green grass. The Department of Agriculture undoubtedly appears to him to be far off and ridiculous as a source of assistance. However, one should never look a gift horse in the mouth. This is particularly true if the horse trots citywards. Although farm products are grown in the country, they are for the most part consumed in the city. This is the link enabling the Agriculture Department to be of assistance to urban dwellers.

The Agricultural Marketing Service administers the Packers and Stockyards Act. This act protects all consumers because it forces those in the interstate meat-and-poultry business to conform to specific health standards. If this were not so, nothing would prevent dishonest merchants from selling diseased or poor-quality meat. The government inspectors attempt to see that this does not occur. Thanks for this protection is due to the congressmen who passed this legislation. Homemakers or groups of homemakers who are not happy with their meat or poultry have a perfect right to call the Agricultural Marketing Service to check on the quality of the goods. It is often said that ghetto customers receive worse meat than the richer suburban housewives. The reason for this is not so much that suburban women have more money. Actually, more often it is the added education that they have that permits them to overcome their shyness and complain effectively when they receive poor quality. If the urban housewife feels ill at ease in this regard, she should contact her neighborhood antipoverty or social service agency and let it be her spokesman. The Agricultural Marketing Service stands ready to protect the customer. However, it is unrealistic to expect it to have the personnel and finances to wage battle singlehandedly. The urban housewife has herself to blame if she does not start this force rolling. Social workers knowing about this agency would be effective as starting points for complaints as well.

Congress had a similar plan in mind when it passed the

Perishable Agricultural Commodities Act. This is also administered by the Agricultural Marketing Service. Here the service is charged with seeing that fresh and frozen vegetables and fresh and frozen fruit live up to industrywide standards. After making an immediate seizure of a rotten fruit or vegetable that has been transported in interstate commerce, the government can institute legal action to block the sale of any meat or vegetable or fruit failing to meet acceptable standards. The Agricultural Marketing Service should not be regarded as merely a witch hunter. At times it serves the worthy purpose of clearing the reputations of companies that are charged falsely with selling inferior products, just as the Pure Food and Drug Administration will do in its area in the proper case.

In addition to a regulatory role, the Department of Agriculture currently is ranging more broadly into giveaway programs of surplus foods. The idea of paying farmers not to plant food crops is of a highly controversial nature in this country. Even if it is justifiable (and this author is not at all convinced of this), there is absolutely no excuse imaginable for not using the excess food that, even with price supports, is presently grown. Permitting it to spoil from lack of use, which happens more than we like to think, is an outrage when the country contains so many cases of underfed people. The Department of Agriculture is trying to remedy this situation with food stamp programs and free school lunch programs. Starvation is a ready-made weapon for revolutionaries. If the government will not feed the starving in our country, revolutionaries will. Whatever their other policies and actions, the Black Panther free-breakfast program in the ghetto is an excellent idea.

The third major role of the Agriculture Department is an educative one. Shoppers can learn what are the best food buys from Agriculture Department announcements and listings. In addition, the Agriculture Department publishes a yearbook and distributes over 200,000 free copies. In it are contained 400 pages' worth of helpful hints on such varied subjects as judging the freshness of coconuts to whether it is more economical to buy rump cuts or rib cuts of meats. Hundreds of worthwhile suggestions are included. Individual social service agencies are missing a great source of assistance to their clients when they fail to use the services and know-how provided by the Department of Agriculture. Everyone eats food and everyone wastes money by buying food in less than truly economic ways. It would be a great help to the urban poor if the Department of Agriculture became a true neighbor and gave a real helping hand. However, only genuine shows of concern by the urban poor will persuade congressmen to giving high priority to funds for Department of Agriculture programs.

The *Department of Commerce* is another shadowy area for most urban poor. The equivocation of ''commerce'' with ''business'' seems to cause reluctance on the part of many to see what this department offers for the betterment of the individual citizen.

Statistics that contain economic facts for a multitude of businesses are published by the Commerce Department for general distribution. All these data are aimed at increasing economic growth in our country. Ask yourself, is your neighborhood or your city living up to its economic potential? If the true facts were known, could more industry with its resulting helpful effect on the local economy be introduced into your area? Not only could more private industries be brought in if they were aware of the economic benefits of the area in question, but the publication of facts can lead to federal projects receiving priority in your area. Facts are important. If slums are as bad as everyone claims, the government should be encouraged to measure and report just how bad they are in order to illustrate to concerned officials the need for immediate action. There are two Commerce Department agencies of special note in this field. One is the Business and Defense Services Administration. This agency studies long-range prospects for ninety major industries. Continued growth for one or more of these industries could indicate a need for added plants in the urban areas bringing benefits for all. The census taken by the Commerce Department once each decade is another informative instrument for which better use could be made if citizens banded together and demanded that this be done.

In cooperation with the Labor Department and the Health,

Education, and Welfare Department, the Area Redevelopment Administration of the Commerce Department is interested in assisting both private corporations and government agencies in obtaining low-interest loans and outright grants to develop communities. The urban poor should make known to their congressmen that they wish to have their fair share of this money and assistance come into their city.

Although it is now a separate cabinet post, the *Department of Transportation* was an offshoot of the Department of Commerce and can be discussed as if it still were in that department. The placement and use of roads and other forms of mass transportation, such as subways and buses, is of great interest to urban dwellers. It remains to be seen what this department will do either on its own or under pressure to assist the poor in the cities.

We ordinarily do not think of the *Department of Defense* as an agency committed to helping the poor. In the main, the system of draft selection has in all too many ways discriminated against the poor in so many instances. However, the recent outcries against the draft have brought many of these inequities to light. This definitely will achieve more equality of treatment for the poor. On the more monetary level, the Department of Defense has a strongly worded and enforced policy that at least 50 percent of all Defense Department purchases of individual items under $2,500 in value must go to small businesses. Possibly a struggling business manned by members of the urban poor could unearth a bonanza under this provision if its existence were known.

Because it should not come as a surprise to anyone, it will be sufficient to assert that the *Department of Health, Education, and Welfare*, more than any other department, is dedicated to solving the problems of the urban poor. This fact having been declared, we can pass on to the specifics of the situation. However, at least one word should be said about the practical impossibility faced by this department. Poverty is everywhere in our country and there are certainly a limitless number of roots responsible for the problem. It is going to take decades, even centuries, to solve poverty, and realistically speaking, when we assess the greed lurking in the hearts of men, poverty may never be truly ended. Therefore, it is insane to expect H.E.W. to end poverty. Still, even a little relief is a great help. It is a shame that it has taken us so long as a nation to arrive at a firm intention to try to make any inroads at all. Along with the vastness of the problem and the lateness of the attempts at cure, it must be realized as well that each professional has a different approach. There are as many ideas for solving poverty as there are potential solvers. The complexity and multiplicity of poverty roots are in large measure responsible for this situation. In addition, H.E.W. is particularly vulnerable to pressure groups, be they charitably or materialistically motivated. Just as "not everyone who cries Lord, Lord, will enter the Kingdom of Heaven," not everyone who seeks to help the poor is motivated by good will. In both areas, frauds abound.

In the health area, the Food and Drug Administration, which is a part of the Department of Health, Education, and Welfare, is a protective agency that seeks to guard the public against hazardous and dangerous substances of many varieties. This agency is consumer-oriented and for this reason standards of safety are set up to which products of this type sold in interstate commerce must conform. As occurred with the Department of Agriculture and its Agricultural Marketing Service, there is the impossibility of keeping ahead of the thousands of new and changing products. Public complaints are absolutely necessary to give leads as to the whereabouts of likely offenders. In recent years, the Food and Drug Administration has been charged with enforcing truth in labeling statutes that have as their purpose alerting the customer to all of the ingredients contained in the products which he uses. This raises the problem of what the customer can do with this information once he obtains it since most of the ingredients are chemical compounds that mean little or nothing to the consumer. This would be a good area for neighborhood agencies to recruit personnel of public health agencies and local medical men to educate the public as to which ingredients have possibly harmful side effects. Ignorance of the possible effects of drugs and foods can cause needless suffering and sickness for all, but especially for the poor who have less access to medical assistance.

The Public Health Service seeks to prevent communicable diseases from occurring and spreading. In addition, it supervises public hospitals and public rest homes and under a little known act, the Hill-Burton Act, it can provide funds for new public hospitals and public rest homes. As with so many other agencies that we have and will examine, the priority of funds is determined by known need. Just as few of us inherit from long-lost, rich relatives, few areas get public health funds (or funds or assistance from any other agency for that matter) if they do not make their need known and actively seek these funds. Rich uncles do not grow on trees in the real world.

An area in which Public Health agencies could make a meaningful contribution for the urban poor is in ridding industries of occupational health hazards. Clearly the factory workers are the urban poor. Although we are out of the dark ages in this regard thanks to the activities of the International Ladies' Garment Workers Union and other socially conscious groups active in the 1930s, more emphasis on improving factory conditions is needed. This is not to say that everyone has to work in a Park Avenue penthouse. However, everyone is entitled at the least to conditions that are not harmful to his health. In conjunction with state and local health departments, the Public Health Service of the Department of Health, Education, and Welfare will cooperate in making suggestions and if necessary in enforcing rules and regulations preventing harm to the health of employees. Again, unless interested individuals and agencies in the cities start the ball rolling, there is little possibility that it will start itself. Since many factory workers are part of the urban poor, they and those interested in their welfare must take the first step to demand that the government agencies in question take the proper steps to improve the conditions which are harmful to the health of these workers.

In the welfare and social security areas, the government is interested in providing advantages and assistance to all with serious needs. In the welfare area, such bureaus as the Children's Bureau and those dealing with the Aging, Juvenile Delinquency, Family Services, and Cuban Refugees are all specialized attempts to control the problem. In like manner, the Vocational Rehabilitation Administration strives to make productive citizens of those disabled, whether of a physical or mental nature. These are important programs that have as their root source for recruitment the urban poor. Close cooperation with these agencies will be of help for all.

The Department of Education is vitally associated with the urban poor. The ghetto school child of today will be the urban poor of tomorrow. Rags-to-riches stories don't often happen in the ghettos. Unless education can raise these people above themselves, intellectual slumism will abound. The early years are, practically speaking, the only chance. This is why it is so important that everything possible be done in this area to make the atmosphere as good as possible for learning and advancement. The United States government appreciates this fact and will either voluntarily or under pressure from voters, if necessary, do everything possible to better the position of these people. This philosophy of service can take on many aspects extending from the obvious ones of total legal integration and meaningful school subjects to in-school health supervision and black studies programs. The educational process cannot change overnight, but it does recognize the problem and is beginning to assemble the wealth and personnel to fight the problem. The outlook is good.

Another federal agency that is prepared to serve the people is the *Department of Justice*. We often think of it as the strong arm of the government that seeks to place wrongdoers in jail. This is certainly true, but its function is wider in scope than this alone. The Antitrust Division of the Attorney General's Office accepts complaints from all citizens concerning price fixing and other monopolistic practices engaged in by corporations in order to make profits at the expense of the public. Although the department has its proverbial ear to the ground and digs out many violations, it will investigate and consider complaints from any outside source. The Federal Trade Commission will also investigate complaints in this area.

The Department of Justice is also equipped and ready to take legal action against advertising and business violations of laws such as the Pure Food, Drug and Cosmetics Act. In addition, complaints concerning violations of the Federal Civil Rights Act of 1964, which prohibits discrimination in public accommodations, public facilities, restaurants, federal voting, and sex discrimination in employment situations, are investigated and, if necessary, prosecuted by the Department of Justice. The Civil Rights Division of the Attorney General's Office and the Community Relations Service, which is part of the Commerce Department, attempt to assist businesses in complying with the provisions of the Civil Rights Act.

The Department of Justice has received great new power from Congress to stamp out drug traffic in this country. The law giving them this authority is the Comprehensive Drug Abuse Prevention and Control Act of 1970, a long title but a fine piece of work that may finally turn the tide in this horrible struggle. If we can wipe out illegal drugs, crime will be reduced significantly and the motivation of many people greatly increased. Stronger punishment for drug pushers and more compassionate treatment for users are needed as well. In addition, congressional pressure to cut off foreign-aid funds to nations that sell opium as a legal product will also help. All community agencies must cooperate in this struggle.

More than almost any other department, it seems necessary today for the Department of Justice to go to the people with proof of its usefulness and real concern with the problems of the poor. The road for revolutionaries is too easy. They should not be given such easy pickings. The system of justice in this country is, given human error, extremely fair and compassionate. It should be made clear to all that the government's only function in the justice area is to be of assistance to the public as it enforces impartially the laws of this country. More than anything else, public belief in the truth of this statement will counter the revolutionary charge that we have a monolithic, selfish, unfeeling government that brutalizes and oppresses the masses as its main ambition. The best way for the government to prove its case is by good works.

One other government department with a great deal of interest in the urban poor is the *Department of Labor*. Next to education, which is geared for help in the future, working opportunities and conditions are the most important method of improvement available to assist the urban poor. In an attempt to be of service, the Department of Labor operates the United States Employment Service in connection with the various state employment agencies. One advantage to this arrangement is that these government agencies charge no fee, whereas private employment agencies do. This means that the governmental employment agencies have as their only goal helping the prospective employee. A private employment agency has as its first goal the making of a profit. Otherwise, it goes out of business. Since its goal is to help the public, the United States Employment Agency should pay great attention to the need of the poor. It can develop new job markets and administer tests to see which skill areas are best for the prospective employee. A private agency which seeks a percentage of the employee's salary from the new position is not financially able to take the time for humanitarianism. Since these are the employment facts of life, they should be recognized as such. The answer is to insist that the government take even a stronger interest in the employment area than it has up to the present. Strong demands should be made on the government and large corporations to train those unable to get positions. Many large corporations, such as Chrysler Motor Company and General Electric, have led the way in employing and training those whom it would otherwise not employ. Results on the whole have been favorable when certain commonsense adjustments are made by the company. The government must encourage this sort of program even more than it has in the past. Tax advantages for helpful corporations might be a good way of doing this.

The Labor Department's assistance to those who earn small salaries extends into many different areas. Since the pay is small, the work is often routine and degrading. Therefore, the Labor Department will conduct close inspections of safety standards and working conditions. Also minimum wage laws are passed and enforced, as are laws stating that women must receive the same pay as men if they do the same work as men and vice versa. The Walsh-Healey Public Contracts Act provides that any company dealing with the government in the public contracts area can have its minimum wage level raised as a condition of doing business with the government. Such a company must pay its employees on federal jobs the same scale of pay as is generally received by employees in the same community operating a similar business. The decision to raise this minimum wage level is up to the Department of Labor.

In conjunction with the Department of Health, Education, and Welfare, the Department of Labor seeks to block suffering that will be caused by automation and tries to either raise the skills or train in a totally different skill those who will be fired because automation makes their further employment unnecessary. Management claims that automation will enable a manufacturer to cut costs and thus charge less for his product. The lower prices will enable more people to purchase more goods. This in turn will cause the wholesaler to hire more men and buy more trucks to process the greater number of goods received from the manufacturer because of the larger retail demand. In the same way, railroad freight business will increase because of the added orders. This will cause the hiring of more men and the purchasing of more railroad cars. Naturally this bright picture painted by management assumes that inflation will be checked and that union demands, taxes, and other costs that must be borne by management will not rise. If these costs rise, the savings to management by automation will at best only cancel the added costs from other areas. If this is so, prices will not drop and the extra sales counted on to aid the economy will not occur. It is a far wiser course to presume that automation will hurt the unskilled and plan ahead for this eventuality. If in fact it turns out that automation does benefit the urban poor, so much the better. The skills learned on the chance that automation would hurt can always be utilized in the better job occasioned by automation. Machines and computers get better all the time. The poor must be protected in this area.

Another Labor Department attempt at solving unemployment and motivating those involved toward seeking better positions in the future is the Neighborhood Youth Corps. This program received a great deal of criticism in the early days of the Johnson administration. The management and spending of funds was often not terribly wise. However, the idea of taking high school dropouts off the street and giving them positions has great possibilities. The involvement with counselors and supervision can lead to a desire to improve skills or ever better to return to school. An offshoot of the thinking behind the Neighborhood Youth Corps has led the Department of Labor into a heavy emphasis and commitment in the summer job market for school-age youth. The goals of the Department of Labor meet their greatest challenge in the ghetto. The assistance of all is needed to bring meaningful work and more importantly, proper work motivation to ghetto dwellers. Collaboration with local churches and other community organizations is the best way to achieve this goal.

In the 1930s, *Rackety Rax*, a delightful, comic novel, was written by Joel Sayre. It concerned a group of mobsters who, after counting the house at a Notre Dame game, started their own university just to have a football team so as to collect large sums from gate receipts. One of the characters passed on some immortal advice on committing crime and not being caught. Three cardinal rules to observe were to stay out of the newspapers, not to kill a cop, and not to mess with the United States mails. Inspectors of the *Postal Service* have a justifiably high reputation for tracking down swindlers and hucksters who utilize the United States mails to defraud the public. There are no available figures as to the amount of fraud carried out through the mails. Nor do any solid figures exist to estimate whether the poor utilize the Postal Inspectors to crack down on this type of swindle as much as their richer counterparts in this country do. However, it is safe to assume that because of the educational and cultural differences, the poor do not utilize this service to the same degree. For the same reason, however, it is clearly true that the poor are more susceptible to this type of fraud. The agencies and workers involved with the urban poor would do their clients a great service if they told them of the availability and willingness to help of the Postal Inspectors. It would give Joel Sayre's advice an opportunity to be proven true. The Postal Inspectors have an office in virtually every main post office building in this country.

The *Department of Housing and Urban Development* has great importance for the city dweller. One important aspect is in an indirect manner as a guarantor of mortgage loans made by banks. This backing encourages banks to make loans to people with a lower financial rating than they usually demand. This is also true if the borrower is a corporation like a neighborhood nonprofit corporation, rather than a single owner. The H.U.D. guaranty encourages housing starts, rest home construction, and the improvement of property. The department is very alert in stamping out bias and racial discrimination in this area.

Urban renewal is a closely related area that has a lot of federal money at its disposal. Much benefit can occur to the poor if urban renewal is intelligently planned. It is vital that the poor participate at all levels of administration and planning from top to bottom. If necessary, groups of urban poor should enforce this right with the help of the courts.

The National Labor Relations Board can be very helpful to the urban poor. It is beyond our scope to discuss specific regulations and forbidden conduct in this field. The basis for federal activity in this area is for the most part an outgrowth of the Taft-Hartley Act and the Landrum-Griffin Act. In addition to these acts, federal agencies such as the National Labor Relations Board and the Federal Mediation and Conciliation Service and the National Mediation Board are of assistance in labor controversies. All of these activities of the government are geared to prevent those who work with their hands from being relegated to little more than the "wetback" class. Almost totally, the urban poor are direct descendants of the Industrial Revolution or of Southern slave plantations. The horrid treatment of the laborer has occurred over and over until the present time.

Unionism in this country has made great strides in lifting the working class to a place of respectability in our society. The struggle has been a bitter one and unions are guilty of many abuses and even crimes. Fault is on both sides. We all know that in too many unions the concept of a fair day's work for a fair day's pay is a joke. Both the leaders who set these policies and the spineless sheep who follow them are to blame. Extended to the ultimate, companies will fall or at least be unjustly hurt. Labor has ignored its duty in this regard to an absolutely disgusting degree in many instances. Possibly the time has come for the federal agencies to bring the balance of power back in the other direction. Helping the poor is one thing, permitting a rape of management is entirely another. At some point justice must prevail. There is much that government and industry can do to help the poor. This should not be seized on by union members to irresponsibly and even criminally exploit the employer. The ironic thing is that slowdowns that are designed to spread the work and thereby benefit all workers have the opposite effect for two reasons. First of all, slowdowns raise the cost of the manufacturer's product. This causes him to raise the retail selling price of the product, which in turn forces the employee to pay more for the product himself. Secondly, 32 million Americans own shares of stock. Slowdowns cut into their own profits. The stupidity of advocating slowdowns has its equal in stupidity in the urban renewal field. Too many citizens demand enormous sums of money from the government for urban renewal projects that are not totally necessary. "The government must give us money for urban renewal!," is the cry. Think for a moment! Who gave the government this money in the first place? Is it not the taxpayer? If taxpayers remembered that it is their own money that is being spent, they might be a lot slower to demand its use for less than totally necessary projects. As demonstrated, if the union worker realized that less than total production on his part hurts himself most, there might be less featherbedding and slowdowns. Balance is badly needed in labor and management dealings. In the long run, violence brings more violence and dishonesty brings more dishonesty and bad treatment brings more bad treatment for labor as much as for management. Square as it seems these days, there is great practical truth in the Golden Rule.

The Small Business Administration is another possible source of assistance to the urban poor that should be investigated thoroughly. It can be of great help to the individual or small group who are trying to start a business. The Small Business Administration can provide loans at low rates, technical assistance, and counseling on new techniques and markets. The classification of a business as "small" is very general and takes in a large percentage of the companies in this country. Naturally, everyone wants to take advantage of this service. This is impossible and priorities must be established. The urban poor should be at the top of this list, just as whenever possible they should be favored in the awarding of government contracts. These are legitimate ways to guarantee effectively that America will be a land of opportunity for all.

Summing up

The number of federal agencies that are connected in some form with the poor makes a rather lengthy list. This is natural since our government in all its aspects represents all of the people and a great many of these people both live in cities and are poor. The same reasoning applies to state and city agencies. An exhaustive list of these would likewise be massive. Many of them will be just as helpful on a local level to the urban poor, as federal agencies will be on a national level. The message of this chapter is to expend every energy to utilize what is available. This is a perfect illustration of the old saying that "a bird in the hand is worth two in the bush." Legislators can be utilized to guarantee that the agencies involved spend the funds already made available to them in the best manner possible.

This chapter has indicated a rarely employed application of "law" to help the urban poor. Laws are the bedrock that erected, staffed, and acted as the financial guideposts for the agency program. All those concerned directly with the urban poor should take advantage of laws already passed and attempt to utilize the know-how and expert advice that employees working for these agencies and cabinet departments possess and are very willing to use to help the poor, if only asked to do so. Both alone and through neighborhood nonprofit agencies, it is time to give some of these government departments a chance to prove themselves.

Chapter 12

Waiting in Your Welfare Line

Setting the scene

Our reason for putting welfare last is that it is the refuse bin of our system. It is the proof that we have not used our legal system. Welfare is impossible. It can't succeed. However, during the time it is necessary, we must attempt to make it as fair and equal as possible.

With the possible exception of the draft into military service, no subject touching the roots of American life brings about as many arguments as does welfare. It would be silly to rush into a prolonged discussion of laws affecting welfare before discussing the root meaning of the term. Actually it is the root meaning of welfare that causes most of the confusion and hard feelings. The laws surrounding welfare are much easier to apply if we get on the right track at the start.

In the spring of 1970 Johnny Cash, a popular singer who fits well the category of "an instant success after 15 years of trying," was going to give a special concert at the White House. In a stunning mistake by an experienced politician, the President requested that Cash include "Welfare Cadillac" in his list of songs. An instant controversy arose. Aside from the fact that Cash refused the request because he never had sung the song before, Mr. Nixon received great criticism for his public recognition of a savage little tale that told the story of a lazy fellow who did no work and lived totally on what the government gave him. He did so well with government handouts that he was able to afford a brand new Cadillac on what was left over. The punch line was that the new President (Nixon) was going to raise welfare payments, so his wife was out looking for her own "Welfare Cadillac." The outcry against this request was so loud that Mr. Nixon hastily withdrew it. Still, the song reflects a philosophy that has many backers in America. Probably Mr. Nixon liked the song more for the indirect reference to him than for the underlying philosophy. Nonetheless, Nixon touched a sensitive nerve. Is welfare no more than an escape for the lazy and shiftless of our society? Or, alternately, does every man have such a basic right to a bearable life that if he is unable to provide it himself, the government must do so for him? In other words, is a welfare recipient taking by right or is he a beggar who receives his allotment at the sole discretion of the government and on the terms that the government imposes?

History of welfare

To attempt any sort of adequate answer to the status of a welfare recipient, it is necessary to approach the problem from a historical perspective. In Roman times, the bread and other tokens tossed out to the crowds were clearly a gift from the aristocrats to the starving poor. No strings were attached, at least not directly. Of course, though a gift, the motivation as so often occurs with a gift was not totally pure. The favor of the crowd was being sought. Those state leaders who gave the most to the poor had the best chance of receiving its support when the inevitable next governmental power struggle occurred.

After the conversion of Constantine to Catholicism in 313 A.D., Catholicism became the official state religion. One of the primary teachings of the Catholic Church was that for an individual to merit eternal salvation in heaven, it was necessary to give to the poor. All the heads of state felt obliged as Catholics to give either personally or through the government to the poor because they desired salvation as individuals. For some government officials, the early equivalent of welfare was an insurance policy for heaven. Of course, unqualified, this statement would be a shocking denial of the highest motives of the state and its rulers in early times that unquestionably often existed. Examples such as Martin of Tours giving half of his cloak to a freezing peasant in the middle of winter and Elizabeth of Hungary depriving herself of food during a famine so that the serfs of her kingdom could eat, occurred throughout Europe's early history.

Therefore, at least until Reformation times in the early seventeenth century, it is fair to say that welfare was strictly a gift on the part of the individuals who controlled the government, regardless of their motive. There was no thought of any right on the part of any welfare recipient to be cared for if he could not do so himself. Any gift toward the poor was strictly discretionary with the state and its rulers. Aid could be cut off without giving a reason at any moment. In fact, a claim by a peasant that he had a right to receive this assistance would be the fastest way of having his funds cut off because he was an ungrateful swine. The end of the Middle Ages and the rise of the merchant class, industrialization, and the separation of state and church to a large extent ended the close alliance between the leaders of the state and the state itself in giving to the poor. Although they both still did so, they no longer did it together. The state's idea was to help the people who were its citizens. Still, the thinking was that this was a gift. The religious motivation for gifts by individuals is left to God to judge. As we passed into the twentieth century, more and more Americans became convinced that the government would take care of them in any event if they could not take care of themselves. From this state of mind, it is a quick mental shift of gears to hold that the government must take care of those in need; and that when they are in need, people have the right to demand assistance.

Right to welfare?

The Social Security Act of 1934 is the first major occasion in which the United States government stated publicly that the recipient had a right to the benefits in question and that more than a gift was intended. There is a large doubt that Congress ever intended for a moment that an enforceable right existed by which the elderly could demand absolutely that they receive benefits. Whether Congress intended this or not, the administrators of the Social Security Program acted as if a real right to this assistance did exist. This was the first foot in the door for welfare rights. In the United States, we say that a man has a right to own property. His house, his clothes, his car, his money are his. This concept of property as belonging to an individual is the opposite of the communist theory that the state owns everything. Anything that an individual has in a Communist country is a gift from the government and can be taken back at any time. In all areas, the government is supreme. In our country, the individual is supreme; and as long as he does not step upon the rights of other individuals, he has a total right to possession of his private property. Only the most overwhelming demonstration of need by the government will justify its taking over the private property of an individual American. Should this overpowering need occur, and the government's power to take property by "eminent domain" is the most outstanding example that comes to mind, the person whose private property is taken must be justly paid for what he lost. No right to be paid for what he lost exists in Communist countries, and in fact, payment does not occur with any regularity. This is based on the theory that what is freely given is freely taken away. Most Communist countries follow this theory literally.

The Federal Social Security Act of 1934 framed the question for the first time as to whether a government payment to private citizens was a property right that they could be described as owning. In the context of the Social Security Act, the important question was whether a person who qualified for social security could demand that the benefits be given to him. Note that this demand is one step beyond the guarantee of equal protection and due process that we talked about in many other areas when the question of the federal government's applying the same criteria for all citizens concerning the action or program in question. The demand for equal protection and due process for all citizens occurred in areas as diverse as providing the opportunity for effective legal counsel for all criminal defendants, to providing for desegregation in schools, to permitting all citizens to vote. This laudable goal of equal protection and due process is only part of what we mean when talking about the right to welfare. Although it's a big assumption, for the present let us assume that all citizens are treated equally under the law in the application of welfare laws. What we are interested in now is whether the government must take care of those in need of assistance. Do you understand the distinction? It is hoped so because it is important. The government could be as equal as possible in its procedures to deal with those receiving welfare. However, what good would it do if the government washes its hands of the problem entirely and refuses to assist any poor person at all; or alternately, reduces drastically all welfare assistance across the board?

In a day when the government financial commitments at home, abroad, and even in the stars are frighteningly expensive, there is fear that a future government should adopt the "every man for himself" attitude and give the poor nothing. However, the loss does not have to be as stark as a total cutoff of welfare funds to a deserving recipient. The whole relationship between a welfare recipient and the government is based on the answer to the question as to whether a welfare recipient has a property right to welfare or does he take it as a gift. In other words, if he is needy, can a citizen say to the government (which is here an extension of all the taxpayers) that you must support me? As an American citizen, I have a property right to support. You must support me. Or alternately, is the welfare recipient placed in the role of a beggar who comes hat in hand and takes what is given to him? Must the welfare recipient fulfill whatever requirements the government sets for qualifying as a recipient and not have a chance to object to the requirements or the amount of assistance it is decided he shall receive? Since 1934, the question of whether welfare is a property right or a gift has been contested a number of times in the courts. Hard as it seems to believe, we really still do not have an answer other than to observe that courts are going to walk a tightrope in each individual case in which they are called upon to answer this question. Anyone who doubts that the Supreme Court is not still stuck on the welfare rights question, has only to read the 1971 case, *Wyman* v. *James,* or the 1972 case, *Richardson* v. *Belcher,* on the question of caseworker visits, to see that it still does not have an answer.

Let us explore this question of the exact nature of welfare a little further. This time we will take a slightly different approach. Is there a necessity to pay back to the government what was received in welfare payments if the recipient later comes into money? We are not talking about any moral obligation that might exist to repay this money. At present, we are concerned only with a possible legal obligation. Can a state say that this money was really a long-term, no-interest loan, and now that you have money, it is time to pay us back? Alternately, can the so-called loan be given as part of a specific contract which the recipient had to sign before receiving any money? Generally this sort of contract demands repayment at a specified time. The welfare recipient can pay back the sum advanced from any source; or alternately, he can work in a job provided by the government and the amount due to the government will be deducted from his wages. If not a loan or a contract, the third possibility is that the money which the government handed over to the welfare recipient became in all respects the money of the welfare recipient the minute he receives it. Let us examine these possibilities in light of two ultimate possibilities that we disscussed earlier, that is, welfare as a gift or as a property right. Either explanation would fit with the idea that the government has no right to demand compensation for the assistance rendered. This of course cannot be carried to the extreme of fraud or mistake.

In those cases the government would be obliged to recover the monetary amount of the assistance they handed out thinking the recipient was in need.

Whether they have held that welfare is a gift or a property right, most American states actually have not attempted to recover for assistance rendered to their poor citizens. California and some of the Southern states have gone the farthest in treating welfare as a right to which poor citizens are entitled in a totally free manner. On the other hand, New York, surprisingly since it has so much taxable revenue, has been the most strict in tracking down any windfalls received by those on its welfare rolls and recovering what it is owed from this amount. The State of New York has done so in situations where this action has had the effect of putting the recipient back in the poverty status from which he had so recently escaped.

Recently, the sort of state action taken by New York has been challenged in the courts. Also the theory that the money in question is given either implicitly or explicitly as a loan demanding repayment has also been challenged. The loan or contract is claimed to be made under force. This seems legitimate when we reflect upon the situation for a minute. In our discussion about annulments of marriages, the idea of the validity of a marriage in which one party was forced against his or her will to participate was discussed. Since one party would not have agreed to the marriage contract unless forced to do so, it was permissible to annul the marriage on the theory that but for the force there would not have been a marriage ceremony. Similar reasoning applies to loans or written contracts to repay welfare assistance. Can one say that the welfare recipient entered into the supposed agreement of his own free will? Probably not. When we reflect upon the terrible living conditions endured by most welfare recipients, it stretches belief to think that they could deal with an unbiased mind concerning any agreement that might bring some relief from the poverty which they must tolerate day by day. In this context, a defense of force assumes validity and accounts for the success that has occurred recently to attacks at state attempts to collect repayment from welfare recipients.

Constitutional protection for welfare recipients

The success at blocking the necessity to repay welfare assistance may be said to be nothing more than bringing to welfare clients the same rights under contract laws as anyone else. This recent success for welfare recipients can be equalled in many other aspects of welfare law. Residency requirements are an outstanding example. It was inevitable that a challenge would occur in this area. Some states are more disposed to giving a higher priority in their budget to welfare payments than other states. The result is that the poor are given more assistance in some states than in others. For this reason, is it surprising that a number of people requiring assistance would shift from state to state, or city to city in order to obtain more benefits from the government? The problem took on extremely serious proportions when some totally hateful, deep-South cities actively encouraged the black poor in their cities to move to the North and thereby swell its welfare responsibility rather than their own. The Southern cities paid for the transportation and moving costs for these unfortunates, who were being treated as mere cattle that could be driven away at will. Naturally the cities and states that were advanced enough to have forward-looking approaches to the welfare problem resented the exploitation of their goodwill, regardless of whether the motivating force for this exploitation was the government of another state or city on the one hand or the scheming of an individual on the other.

To block the practice of shopping around to find the best possible area for welfare benefits, some programs established residency requirements as a basis for eligibility. These regulations were often worded in such a manner that it was necessary to reside in the state or city in question for a year before becoming eligible for assistance. Obviously, residency requirements would discourage welfare forum shopping and tend to keep the welfare resident tied to the original state. Usually the recipient would reason that it is preferable to receive a continuous smaller amount from the original state than to receive nothing for a year in the new state before being eligible for higher amounts of public assistance. Could a state legally make such a residence requirement? The United States Supreme Court eventually said no when a case challenging a welfare residency requirement came before it for hearing and decision. The United States Supreme Court struck down residency requirements as a violation of the privileges and immunities clause of the United States Constitution in the 1969 case, *Shapiro* v. *Thompson*. A residency requirement was held to be a severe block to the absolute right to move from state to state enjoyed by all the citizens of the United States.

A problem equal in importance to that of residency requirements was substitute-father statutes. State welfare departments were concerned that women who were receiving assistance because they lived alone with their children were actually living with a man who should be responsible for the support of the woman with whom he shared bed and board. This obligation to support the woman would carry over to her children as well. Efforts to force the man to support the woman and children were made by denying women in such a situation any welfare assistance. Legal challenge was made and the United States Supreme Court eventually struck down this type of denial of assistance as being a violation of the equal protection clause of the Constitution.

Clearly if a welfare recipient can challenge residency requirements and substitute father-statutes to name but two, we are not talking about a gift. Welfare is not a gift if a recipient can defy regulations established by the giver and still be eligible for aid. A true gift implies that a giver sets all the conditions. Although it is clear that welfare is not strictly a gift, is it, therefore, a right? We cannot say so on the evidence of the Supreme Court striking out residency requirements and substitute-father statutes. Both decisions can be and indeed should be thought of as holding that if the government does decide to make benefits available to poor citizens, it must do so in such a manner that the constitutional rights of the recipients are not taken away from them. This stops short of saying that the government must assist those of its residents not capable of taking care of themselves financially.

For two weeks in March of 1970, advocates of welfare as a property right felt that after thrity-six years of waiting, the promise of a right to welfare that was hinted at in the administration of the Social Security Act of 1934 had finally come true. The cause for this hope was provided by the United States Supreme Court decision in the *Kelly* case. In a five-to-three decision, it held that a man who was already receiving welfare could not be deprived of it without the government giving the citizen the chance to use all his constitutional rights (e.g., due.process and equal protection) to fight the loss of benefits. This was a large step in the direction of saying that the government must always provide needy citizens with assistance. If this were so, it would strengthen the authority of all the demands that welfare recipients would make in the future. For two weeks, this seemed to be true until the Supreme Court decided the *Dandridge* and *Rosado* cases.

The exact question covered in the *Rosado* case concerned the right of a state to reduce the amount of welfare payments to some individuals and families by lumping together different items and consolidating these subjects into statistical averages. This could result in a reduction of aid to individual families whose specialized needs would not be dealt with separately in the future. The United States Supreme Court permitted this type of averaging as long as it stayed within the broadest interpretation of equal protection structures. *Dandridge*, the other case decided with *Rosado*, permitted a state to give a specified maximum amount to each family eligible for welfare even though this would have the practical effect of excluding certain eligible individuals from receiving any payment at all. In the State of Maryland, where the Dandridge family resided, no payment was made for a seventh child or any individual child after six for that matter. This state regulation was challenged as being discriminatory against large families. The United States Supreme Court did not seem overly concerned as long as each eligible family received some assistance.

In both *Rosado* and *Dandridge,* the Supreme Court applied a balancing-of-interests test that it had first proposed in *Kelly.* This standard was set forth as being "the extent to which (the theoretically aggrieved would-be recipient) may be condemned to suffer grievous loss, and depends on whether the recipient's interest in avoiding that loss outweighs the governmental interest. . . ." In the *Rosado* and *Dandridge* cases, the interest of the government was believed to be more important by the United States Supreme Court. This in effect pulled the rug out from under the idea of the welfare recipient's property right in receiving assistance that seemed to have been asserted by the Supreme Court in *Kelly* only two weeks before.

As a result of the important cases decided in the welfare area in the spring of 1970, *Kelly, Rosado,* and *Dandridge,* it is safe to say that as to being a property right, welfare is somewhere between the devil and the deep blue sea. The individual welfare recipient does not have a right to the reception of assistance, but on the other hand the government does not have the total right to cut off or reduce this assistance whenever it feels like it. Welfare is not a gift and not a property right. It is submitted that in the long run this is a much better position for both the best interests of the government and those of the individual recipient. Before the reader jumps to the incorrect conclusion that the author is not in favor of the government assisting those who cannot subsist on their own, it should be asserted that he is. However, he is disturbed at what he senses to be a growing acceptance in American society of welfare being a positive good. This idea he does not agree with at all.

Legal assistance in the welfare area

When talking about the availability of welfare assistance, it is absolutely necessary to distinguish between the short run and the long run. How long you define short and long can differ. Whether you say the short run is five, ten, twenty, or even thirty years, there must come a time in the future when one says that welfare must end and that continuance past this point would be a positive harm to society and its members. This is stated because the reality of public assistance has a very bad effect on society as a whole and the individual recipient in particular. It is degrading to have another take care of you. It kills initiative and reduces productivity. Possibly there is some justification for this sort of dependence in a less highly developed society than our own when such dependence is not absolutely necessary.

It is interesting to note that Russia and many of its satellites are slowly moving away from the concept of a managed society toward the concept of capitalism and individual initiative. This is being done in these countries at the loss of a great deal of personal face, since the need for a managed society was the original reason for their very existence. However, they have come to realize that their country is better off in the long run if the individual initiative of a capitalistic society is emphasized.

One can say it is all well and good to praise individual initiative, but millions of Americans are locked into a stranglehold of poverty, disease, and illiteracy. With this we must agree. Obviously, we must mount all our weapons in an attempt to end this condition. During this period of "war against poverty," to employ a favorite political cliché, we must aid those in need to the best of our ability. This is the short run to which we refer. It is hoped that President Nixon's Family Assistance Program is given a fair chance to be judged on its merits and not just on politics. However, we must not lose sight of the forest for the trees. The light at the end of the forest, however dim it may be, is that poverty will end and that further welfare assistance will not be necessary. When the fight over welfare property rights takes on too much importance, the real fear exists that governmental welfare assistance will be treated as regular monetary supplements in a person's pocket that he will not part with under any circumstances. This theory we cannot approve of; and we become very nervous with the tactics of poverty lawyers and social planners who spend so much effort at nailing down the right to assistance for the poor that they appear to lose sight of, or in any way to work for, the long-range goal. Welfare assistance will be a success in this country only when the need for the welfare assistance which these lawyers and social planners so vigorously seek to secure permanently becomes nonexistent.

There are striking resemblances between lawyers, social workers, and social planners who deal with those in stark poverty and doctors who treat patients who are ill with an incurable disease. The doctor tries to lessen the pain and suffering of his patients because they are human beings who deserve as much consideration as possible even though it is clear that there is no hope for their life. Of course, no doctor desires cases like this; and all hope that the day will come when incurable illnesses such as cancer have been solved. Then he can spend his time in treating curable diseases. All doctors hope for the day when all illnesses are curable. In the same way, the lawyer or social worker who deals with poverty clients must hope and work for the day when the poverty cancer is ended. In the meantime he should use all the "medicine" at his disposal to make the suffering of those suffering from poverty as light as possible.

It is within this area of making the suffering of poverty clients as light as possible that the application of constitutional principles occurs. If we must have welfare, and in the previously mentioned short run there is no doubt that we must, the necessity of making the application of the "medicine" in question as much in keeping with "equal protection" and "due process" as possible becomes evident. This short-range approach to welfare is better served by a balancing of interests between the government and the recipient than would be a property-right approach to that which in the long run would be a crutch. It is horrid that we must talk about ten, twenty, or thirty years as a short-run time for ending poverty. However, the world has not succeeded in solving this problem in over 7,000 years of organized existence. It is a great tribute to America that it seriously exists as a possibility that this country can find the solution to poverty during this century.

In this chapter we have used the term government rather interchangeably when talking about welfare programs on a city, state, or federal level. This was done because much intermingling exists especially as to funds. The cost of welfare is so prohibitive that many states have taken over the responsibility from individual towns and cities in order to reduce the administrative costs. This move will be of some benefit to the taxpayer, although what he saves in local property taxes must usually then go into paying an increased state tax levy. Whether the local dispensing agent for welfare funds is the city or the state, most of the funds come from the treasury of the federal government. Actually, as we have seen from our discussion on urban renewal, this money is originally that of all the taxpayers. In most states at least half of the welfare expense is assumed by the federal government as long as the state in question complies with a set of conditions set forth by the federal government to insure that the programs they assist are truly of help to all those eligible. Most welfare disputes end up in federal court as a result of the federal assistance rendered to the states, or on account of the specific language of the Fourteenth Amendment to the United States Constitution, or also by way of Section 1983 of Volume 42 of the United States Code, which allows citizens to sue in federal court those state officials acting illegally under the protection of state law. Before one gets the idea that Section 1983 will provide an open invitation to sue every state or city judge, policeman, or administrator who takes an action with which an individual disagrees, it should be pointed out that federal courts are very closedfisted in their approach to this statute. Application has been rigid and recoveries few.

One federal regulation in the welfare assistance area that has been of great interest is the requirement that a welfare recipient must have counsel appointed for him and paid for him by the state if he so wishes, when he challenges a welfare department ruling against him. This type of hearing is known as a "fair hearing." The *Kelly* case held that a welfare recipient's right to assistance cannot be withdrawn without a hearing in which the constitutional protections guaranteed

to the individual recipient are respected. The federal government regulation that called for the provision of legal counsel
in "fair hearings" was handed down before the *Kelly* case.
In addition, as we recall from our discussion of *Gideon*, it
is only necessary for the government to make legal counsel
available for those who cannot afford it in criminal cases.
So we are not talking about a constitutional guarantee, but
a rather desirable state of affairs in precisely the same manner
that it is desirable to have attorneys available to represent
any poor person wishing such assistance in civil cases. In
the *Kelly* case, the United States Supreme Court so strongly
emphasizes the need for attorneys in these hearings that it
is most likely they will fit this under the constitutional right
to counsel if the government doesn't provide for these attorneys
on its own initiative.

Opposition to assigning counsel in "fair hearings" was
strong enough so that the original target date of July 1, 1970,
has been postponed indefinitely. The difficulty of the task
involved is some justification for the indefinite postponement.
Few areas of the country have legal assistance programs capable of dealing with such added requests for service. The
two fields of housing and domestic relations are enough to
keep most legal aid agencies so well occupied that they have
no time or resources available to engage in such necessary
activities as attempting to promote legal reform and education
of the poor as to their legal rights, to say nothing of such
a vast area as providing representation on request for any
welfare recipient who demands a "fair hearing" for any conceivable reason. The government will have to increase funds
for these agencies; or alternately, pay private attorneys who
agree to handle these cases. In any event, this will be a most
expensive proposition full of technicalities.

A solution proposed by some to the problem of finding
a sufficient number of legal advisors for "fair hearings" is
to have the burden assumed either by law students or by
specially trained laymen. There is something to be said for
this, but either solution is tricky because a little knowledge
is a dangerous thing. To most recipients, whoever represents

them will stand in their minds as a legal opinion to value in all situations. It is feared that unless a tight check is kept on the law student or layman, they will wander off into giving opinions in areas in which they have no legal competence. This could be a real harm if their advice is followed and is incorrect as it well may be.

It does seem that on the whole there is an undeniable need for some type of legal assistance for welfare "fair hearings." To the welfare recipient a small financial difference can be of crucial importance in his attempt to reach a subsistence level. If the complaint is one common to many recipients (e.g., nothing is permitted for Christmas presents for the children), it should be arranged that the equivalent of a "class action" could be filed and all would be bound by the result. This would eliminate the need for separate hearings when many welfare recipients have the same complaint based on a single policy decision.

The welfare "fair hearing" system is a dreadful hodgepodge of inconsistencies, needless complications and duplications, discrimination, and unnecessary variability in the application of criteria upon which decisions are made. In most states referees who hear the appeals by the welfare recipients are not lawyers. This automatically guarantees less than a uniform application of standards. Often the standards are not clear. In addition, in most states there is a built-in conflict of interest since the referee who decides whether to allow the claim of the welfare recipient is almost always an employee of the state welfare department, one of the adversaries in the case. At least indirectly, pressure must exist for the referee to rule in favor of the department in close cases. If one doubts this, ask yourself realistically that if two referees have a chance for promotion and their qualifications are relatively equal, do you think that the man who finds for his agency in a substantially lower percentage of cases will be promoted? Probably not.

At least arguably, the hearing officer-referee should be an independent third party not dependent on the state welfare agency for his paycheck. Employment of attorneys in private practice as referee-hearing officers would appear to be a most satisfactory solution, especially if the recipient will have easy access to any attorney to argue his case for him. There would not be the pressure of being an employee of one of the parties in the case if the referee-hearing officer were an attorney in private practice. A lawyer would know the law and be able to adopt legal reasoning in arriving at the solution to the dispute. This would go a long way toward eliminating the arbitrariness in decision making that plagues these hearings at the present time. In addition, the employment of attorneys would involve more attorneys in the welfare process. This is all to the good because it is believed that once they experience at first hand the needless red tape of the system, they will strive to reduce the complexity to a workable level. When this is accomplished, the arbitrariness that is an inevitable by-product of complexity and confusion should be reduced as well.

The long-range answer to the problem of providing attorneys for welfare recipients who desire to have legal representation in "fair hearings" seems to lie in the main in perfecting and simplifying the appeal system as much as possible. One of the causes for the great complexity in welfare administration has been that parts of it are all over the place. Within the bounds of justice and charity, it is simply not possible to erect a separate welfare policy for each individual recipient. There comes a point at which general norms must be employed to decide the cases. Administrative efficiency can tolerate nothing else. More general norms are needed in the welfare area so that many cases can be handled at once since the point in issue will be the same. When this administrative restructuring occurs, as it positively must, there will be the real possibility of reducing the number of appeals requiring the services of a separate legal representative to a workable number. If this administrative overhauling does not occur, there is no way that agencies will be able to handle these cases. Administrative restructuring must come.

If administrative restructuring occurs in welfare agencies, the problem of legal representation in "fair hearings" can probably be resolved. A more serious procedural problem is starting to arise that will be harder to resolve. When a welfare recipient protests a reduction in payment, the question as to whether he should receive payment at the original higher rate or at the new objected-to lower rate while he appeals the reduction is yet to be settled. The *Kelly* case said that if the welfare recipient is successful in his appeal, he must be paid the amount of benefits deprived him during the period that he received either none or a reduced amount. The Department of Health, Education, and Welfare's regulation that called for "fair hearings" in all state or local welfare programs drawing upon federal funds specified that benefits could not be reduced or terminated while an appeal is on the books. This provision was objected to by many officials charged with the operation of state and local programs. The feeling was that this freeze provision could be employed by certain unscrupulous welfare recipients so as to stay at the higher unnecessary wage level for an almost indefinite period. This could be done by using all the appeal procedures that are provided, even bringing an unworthy case to the United States Supreme Court, if necessary and possible. Now this is not to stop those who honestly feel an agency ruling is unfair to them from pursuing all the avenues of legal appeal open to them. On the other hand, when one considers that a policy of massive legal resistance could clog the courts for years, abuse is possible.

Yet on the other hand, is it right for the welfare agency to be able to pay the lesser amount during the time before the appeal is decided? If the agency is wrong in its decision, this could work such a great hardship on the recipient and his family that even the payment of the amount held up would not make up for what was lost. A compromise must be worked out that will be fair both to the taxpaying public and to the appealing welfare recipient in question.

Mental health commitments

The nightmares that are common in the administration of welfare programs are just as likely to occur in the area of mental health commitments. Many times the subject in need of state in-patient mental health assistance is also a welfare recipient. This is so because those who can afford private mental health care are usually very quick to seek it because of the bad reputation (only partially deserved) connected with state mental health institutions. Because there is a waiting list for space in state institutions, the state agencies involved in recommending commitment often tend to become a little careless in observing the procedural rights of a citizen when they are able to find an open place in a state institutuion. With rare exception the person in question needs assistance and is fortunate to get it, and the motive of the state agency is to be helpful; however, the agency employees cannot forget that this is still a citizen who must have the opportunity either personally or through the representation of an attorney to contest the need to be committed, if he so wishes.

A further side of the problem with mental health commitments is that people have been committed to state institutions who could have been treated just as adequately on an outpatient basis at a state facility near their home. How is the person involved able to know about these opportunities? It is very hard to place the burden on him alone. Too often the judge charged with deciding whether commitment is necessary has felt that the person in front of him needed some help; and the judge was afraid that if he did not commit him, the man would get no help at all, and that his condition might worsen significantly because of the lack of any care. The only question before the judge was commitment or not and he almost always decided in favor of commitment.

A forward-thinking Federal District Court in the District of Columbia has attempted to solve this problem. So far its solution has not been applied elsewhere, but if adopted elsewhere, it would be a great help to eliminating the "devil or the deep blue sea" approach between commitment and noncommitment that has existed up to the present. The theory behind what is called the *Lake* approach is that the court with the help of both the state and the person opposing commitment should explore all the possible alternatives to total in-patient commitment. As with so many other subjects to which reference has been made in this book, ignorance of programs that do exist is a large defect in the mental health field as well. If the courts demand that all information in this field be collected and made available to the court in making its decison, the chance of overlap and less than total utilization of available services would be minimized. The *Lake* approach could easily be applied to drug addiction commitments and mental health treatment for prisoners as well. It is hoped that it would be adopted on a rather universal scale.

Summing up

At the present time, the need for welfare assistance seems to be never ending and a chapter on this problem could also go on and on. However, the principles outlined in this chapter would be of more assistance if applied rather than talked about. Welfare is a long-range problem; and while it lasts, those citizens who find it necessary to seek welfare assistance must be treated with the same respect and dealt with under the same set of laws as other Americans. This does not mean we should idolize welfare, accept its permanence, or abandon the fight to bring the necessity for it to an end. Welfare assistance is similar to using the drug methadone to treat drug addiction. It helps, but it brings on a dependence of its own. It is a help but hardly a cure. The same is true for welfare assistance.

Urban Law attempts to end welfare. Whether it will succeed or not, we do not yet know. One thing is sure: If it does not, revolution will. Every revolution in history has fed on the hopes of the poor. Welfare takes away hope. Without it, the poor will seek hope in a new system. To block this, we must change our system, and the way to do this? You guessed it! Urban Law.

Afterword

As promised in the first chapter, we have attempted to sketch the outline of an approach that applies legal principles to the problems of the poor. This was done because the subject is too large to pretend that answers exist to solve all or even many of the problems faced currently by the urban poor. It is the message of this book that only through constant faithful application of legal principles will this country be able to solve the problems of the urban poor. As the Declaration of Independence said so well:

> . . . We hold these truths to be self-evident, that all men are created equal, that they are endowed by their Creator with certain unalienable rights, that among these are Life, Liberty and the pursuit of Happiness. —That to secure these rights Governments are instituted among men deriving their just powers from the consent of the governed. —That whenever any form of Government becomes destructive of these ends, it is the Right of the People to alter or to abolish it, and to institute new Government laying its foundation on such principles and organizing its powers in such form as to them shall seem most likely to effect their Safety and Happiness.

Has the time come for the people of this country to say to themselves that the republic that has governed it for nearly two hundred years cannot truly bring "Life, Liberty and the pursuit of Happiness" to the governed; and that they should overthrow this government and bring forth a new one? Has America under its present form of government reached the point where, like the phoenix bird of Egyptian mythology, it is necessary to destroy itself by throwing itself into the fire and then rise again for a new life? If America does destroy itself like the phoenix, will the form of government that takes the place of the present form of government be an improvement; young, clean, and renewed like the phoenix? The answer is a clear and resounding, no! The problem is not with the form of government but its application. The legal formulas exist to guarantee "Life, Liberty and the pursuit of Happiness" to all Americans, rich or poor, white or black, if the individual American citizen wishes that his representatives govern the nation so that these fundamental guarantees are secured for all our citizens. As Cassius observed in Shakespeare's *Julius Caesar*, "the fault dear Brutus lies not in our stars, but in ourselves, that we are underlings."

We are all guilty of blaming the government for faults that we actively encourage by constantly electing representatives whose actions encourage the continuance of the unsatisfactory mode of conduct. A statement of George Washington's in this regard has great validity: "Reason and experience both forbid us to expect that national morality can prevail in exclusion of religious principle." It would be wrong to write this off as a holy catch phrase like "the family that prays together stays together" (although there is a lot of truth to that). Washington and many of the early leaders of this country were anything but churchgoing men, yet they strongly affirmed the existence of God and the need for a code of morality. In our country today, we are so quick to blame the government for faults that are of our causing and responsibility. The situation resembles the scriptural observation that we are much quicker to pluck out the cinder in our neighbor's eye than the beam in our own.

The form of government which America employs provides a way to right wrongs by use of the ballot box. If the citizenry is not happy with the performance of their elected representatives, they should oust them at the next election and replace them with a new group that will fulfill their wishes. This procedure has the blessings of order, peace, and respect for the rights of others. This is the best way to show the will of the governed. Strikes, riots, lockouts, and other forms of violence deny to those opposed to pressure tactics the chance to be governed by majority vote. Instead, they are governed by those willing to employ force. The elected representatives of all the people must protect the orderly governed who wish to be ruled by their elective representatives. They cannot allow a violence-prone minority to impose its rule on the governed. As Father Theodore Hesburgh, the President of Notre Dame University, observed in a *U.S. News and World Report* interview concerning violence in the colleges and universities:

> The argument goes—or has gone: Invoke the law and you lose the university community. My only response is that without the law you may well lose the university and, beyond that, the larger society that supports it and that is most deeply wounded when law is no longer respected, bringing an end of everyone's most cherished rights.

The plea to use the law against violent dissenters must be read in the context that nonviolent dissent is not only protected but even encouraged in our country. The key word is "violent." If every garbage collector or policeman goes on strike in a city, they are denying all the people the right to a clean or safe city. This is violence. If students prevent others from coming on to a college campus, this is violence because it denies access to a public facility to those who desire legitimately the use of the facility. Actions such as this are violent as much as hurling bombs and firing guns. Although the harm is not as immediate, the consequences affect far more people than does direct violence. Nonviolent dissent in the true form relies on the violence of ideas. If enough people agree, they will use the ballot box to express their approval and demand a change. Only in this way can a democracy succeed.

Even if we can reorder our society so that the will of the

majority and the peaceful expression of the desires of dissenters can coexist, there must be a consolidation of our country's goals. This is a marvelous first step. Peace, racial harmony, abolition of poverty, sickness, and discrimination have taken their rightful place in the hearts of Americans. Yet, we cannot succeed in bringing all these dreams to fruition instantaneously. The government is too big and widespread. Discipline is lacking. Almost everyone is well motivated, but no one knows where to start or where to go. False prophets arise. What are called "new ideas" are all around. Yet, too often hot air and expense far outstrip practicality. Our nation is like a chicken with its head cut off, running in nine different directions at once. Leadership must arise that is responsible, experienced, and realistic. Sensible, attainable goals must be established and more importantly be recognized as such, supported and encouraged by the citizenry at large. Programs that are duplications must be ruthlessly suppressed and programs which fail must be eliminated, and those which are directly connected with the true goals must not be postponed. Planning of such a concentrated type is not easy, but is so necessary. There are at present too many agencies, too many programs, and too large a number of nonessential employees. It is necessary to stop the random casting of darts and make fewer, more concerted thrusts against the evil of poverty.

The tone of this book has been for the most part restrained. Too many nasty words have been hurled, too many riots have occurred, too many needless statements have been made. This book has had three main themes. The first was that the American form of government is the best ever conceived by mankind; second, that the way to make needed adjustments in the system is by the peaceful means set forth in the documents of the system; and third, that today America is ashamed of poverty and wishes to have it come to an end. It is the hope of the author that if the reader would not accept any or all of these presuppositions before he started reading this book, he might do so now.

There is no better way to end than once more to call upon

Thomas Jefferson. This time the quote is from Jefferson's first inaugural address:

> If there be any among us who wish to dissolve this union, or to change its republican form, let them stand undisturbed, as monuments of the safety with which error of opinion may be tolerated where reason is left free to combat it. I know indeed that some honest men have feared that a republican government cannot be strong; that this government is not strong enough. But would the honest patriot, in the full tide of successful experiment, abandon a government which has so far kept us free and firm on the theoretic and visionary fear that this government, the world's best hope, may, by possibility, want energy to preserve itself. I trust not. I believe this, on the contrary, the strongest government on earth.

BASIC BIBLIOGRAPHY

BOOKS

Samuel Beers and Richard Barringer, *The State and the Poor,* Harvard University Press, Cambridge, Mass., 1970.

C. A. Bersani, *Crime and Delinquency,* Macmillan Co., London, 1970.

Clearinghouse Review, Northwestern University Law School, Evanston, Ill.

David A. Danelski, *A Supreme Court Judge is Appointed,* Random House, New York, 1964.

Jack Greenberg, *Race Relations and American Law,* Columbia University Press, New York, 1959.

John H. Lambert, *Crime, Delinquency, and Race Relations in Birmingham,* Oxford University Press, London, 1970.

Law Project Bulletin: The National Housing and Economic Development Articles Law Project, Earl Warren Legal Institute, Berkeley, California.

Anthony Lewis, *Gideon's Trumpet,* Random House, New York, 1964.

Charles A. Reich, *The Greening of America,* Random House, New York, 1970.

Henry Rottschaefer, *The Constitution and Socio-Economic Change,* University of Michigan Press, Ann Arbor, Michigan, 1948.

William Ruder and Raymond Nathan, *The Businessman's Guide to Washington,* Prentice-Hall, Englewood Cliffs, New Jersey, 1954.

ARTICLES

Subject	Author	Source
Narcotics Addiction	Arnowitz	67 Columbia Law Review pp. 405-429.
Child Abuse	Paulsen	67 Columbia Law Review pp. 1-49.
Illegitimacy	Krause	44 Texas Law Review pp. 829-859.
Slumlords	Sax	65 Michigan Law Review pp. 869-922.
Sex Discrimination	Miller	51 Minnesota Law Review pp. 877-897.
Public Welfare	Graham	43 New York University Law Review, pp. 451-496.
Juvenile Delinquency	Alper	34 Albany Law Review pp. 46-48.
Courtroom Procedure	Holz	50 Marquette Law Review pp. 450-522.
Mental Health Commitments	Parker	4 Family Law Quarterly pp. 81-89.
	Aron	13 Howard Law Review pp. 303-313.